XUANZANG'S JOURNEY TO INDIA

玄奘西天取经

常 征 著

Translated by LiLi & Wang Wenliang

China Intercontinental Press

图书在版编目（CIP）数据

玄奘西天取经：汉英对照／常征著；李莉，王文亮译．—北京：五洲传播出版社，2010.1
ISBN 978-7-5085-1740-7

I．①常… II．①李… ②王… III．①汉语－对外汉语教学－语言读物 ②玄奘（602~664）－生平事迹－汉、英 IV．①H195.5 ②B949.92

中国版本图书馆CIP数据核字（2009）第207538号

中外文化交流故事丛书（Roads to the World）

总　策　划：	许　琳
策　　　划：	马箭飞　孙文正　王锦红
顾　　　问：	赵启正　沈锡麟　潘　岳
	周黎明（美）　李　莎（加）　威廉·林赛（英）
出　版　人：	荆孝敏　邓锦辉
编　著　者：	常　征
翻　　　译：	李　莉　王文亮
项目统筹：	邓锦辉
责任编辑：	王　峰
设计指导：	田　林
封面绘画：	李　骐
设计制作：	北京原色印象文化艺术中心
图　　　片：	Fotoe　萧　亮　赵文平

玄奘西天取经
Xuanzang's Journey to India

出版发行　五洲传播出版社（北京市海淀区北小马厂6号　邮编：100038）
电　　话　8610-58891281（发行部）
网　　址　www.cicc.org.cn
承　印　者　北京外文印务有限公司
版　　次　2010年1月第1版第1次印刷
开　　本　720×965毫米 1/16
印　　张　11
定　　价　80.00元

Contents 目 录

Foreword *4*

I. Xuanzang and *the Journey to West* *8*

II. Earlier Experience of Xuanzang *16*

III. Stealthily Cross the Border for Buddhist Scriptures *32*

IV. Hardship and Dangers in the Journey to West *48*

V. Study in India *88*

VI. Eloquent Chinese Master *118*

VII. Eastward Return from a Pilgrimage for Buddhist Scriptures *148*

前　言 *6*

1. 玄奘与《西游记》 *9*

2. 玄奘的早期经历 *17*

3. 偷渡国境的取经人 *33*

4. 西行路上多艰险 *49*

5. 留学印度 *89*

6. 雄辩的中国法师 *119*

7. 取经东归 *149*

FOREWORD

It has been a long and exciting history of tremendous cultural exchange between China and other countries. In terms of culture, economy, ideology, and personnel, these exchanges between China and other countries can be dated back to the times of Qin and Han dynasties—directly or indirectly, by land or sea. The long-term and multi-faceted cultural exchange helps the world to understand more about China and the rest of the world, enriching the common wealth of mankind—both materially and spiritually.

The book series entitled *Roads to the World* offers the most splendid stories in the entire history of Sino-foreign cultural exchange. We hereby offer them to foreign students learning the Chinese language, and to foreign readers who have a keen interest in Chinese culture. These stories depict important personalities, events, and phenomena in various fields of cultural exchange between China and other nations, and among different peoples. By reading the books, you may understand China and Chinese civilization profoundly, and the close link between Chinese civilization and other civilizations of the world. The books highlight the efforts and contributions of Chinese people and Chinese civilization in the world's cultural interchange. They reflect mankind's common spiritual pursuit and the orientation of values.

  The book tells stories of Xuanzang, dignitary of Tang Dynasty, about his pilgrimage to the west (India) for the Buddhist scriptures based on the historical records. About 1,400 years ago, the Chinese monk made a great cultural trip and covered hundreds of thousands of kilometers in 17 years despite of numerous difficulties and dangers. He left rich legacy on thought and culture and became a symbol of China-India cultural exchange. The real stories he visited Xinjiang, Middle Asia and India were thrilling with unique charms.

前　言

中国与其他国家、民族之间的文化交流具有悠久而曲折的历史。在中国与外国之间，通过间接的和直接的、陆路的和海路的、有形的和无形的多种渠道，各种文化、经济、思想、人员方面的交流，可以上溯至秦汉时代，下及于当今社会。长期的、多方面的交流，增进了中国与其他国家、民族之间的了解，使人类的共同财富（物质的和精神的）更加丰富。

中外文化交流故事丛书（Roads to the World）的宗旨，是从中外文化交流的历史长河中，选择那些最璀璨的明珠，通过讲故事的方式，介绍给学习汉语的外国学生和对中国文化感兴趣的外国读者。这些故事描述中国与其他国家、民族在各个领域文化交流中的重要人物、事件和现象，以使外国读者能够更深入地理解中国，理解中国文明，理解中国文明与其他各文明之间的密切关系，以及中国人和中国文明在这种交流过程中所作出的努力和贡献，并尽力彰显人类共同的精神追求与价值取向。

  本书依据有关历史记载，讲述唐代高僧玄奘远赴西天（印度）取经的故事。在近1400年前，这位中国僧人不畏艰险，跋涉数万公里，历时17年，进行了一次伟大的文化之旅。他为后人留下了丰富的思想和文化遗产，并成为中印文化交流的象征。他游历新疆、中亚、印度一带的真实故事，别具魅力。

I

Xuanzang and *the Journey to West*

With wizardly imagination, interesting episodes and distinctive roles, *the Journey to West*, published in the 16th century in China, is very popular among readers of different nationalities as a renowned classical work with world influence. The fiction tells the story of the pilgrimage of Tangseng (Tang Monk) to the west (India) for the Buddhist sutras under protection of his three disciples, Sun Wukong (Monkey King) and others. The tale includes 81 adventures in the journey.

The leading role of the story is Sun Wukong, or the Monkey King. Intelligent and brave, the Monkey King is capable of different transformations with an immense amount of strength, and access to the heaven and the hell. He can defeat demons and monsters. Therefore the English translation of the fiction is *Monkey*. By contrast, Tangseng is overshadowed by the Monkey King. Though the fiction describes his honesty, goodness and gut against difficulties

1

玄奘与《西游记》

16世纪时问世的中国神魔小说《西游记》，以神奇的想象、丰富有趣的情节和鲜明的人物形象而受到各国读者喜爱，成为一部具有世界性影响的古典名著。这部小说描写佛教僧人唐僧在孙悟空等三个徒弟的保护下，不远万里、历经81次艰难险阻到西天求取佛经的故事。西天就是现在的印度。

小说的主人公是机智勇敢的猴王孙悟空。他千变万化，法力高强，可以上天入地，降魔伏怪。因此，这部小说的英译本就叫《猴》。相形之下，唐僧的形象则不免逊色，小说虽然也表现了他诚

唐僧师徒塑像，新疆吐鲁番
Statues of Tangseng and his disciples, Turpan, Xinjiang.

for the Buddhist sutras, readers will see more a weak, incapable, pedantry and muddle-headed Buddhist disciple in the fiction. With *the Journey to West* and picture books, films and TV plays, the image of Tangseng and the story of pilgrimage have become household names.

However, Tangseng is not a complete imaginary figure. Tangseng means the monk from the Emperor Tang Dynasty (618–907). In history Tangseng refers to dignitary Xuanzang (602–664). He was a great traveler, translator and Buddhist scholar. Nearly 1,400 years ago, he covered thousands of kilometers in 17 years to India for the Buddhist sutras with unswerving faith, indomitable will and outstanding wisdom. It was a miracle.

Xuanzang's west journey was also a great cultural journey. He wrote the famous historical and geographic book *On Yuan Chwang's Travels in India*, which record the geography, history, customs, products, religion, culture and politics of 110 city-states, regions and countries that he covered and 28 others that he heard about. The book included the famous Bamiyan Buddha of Afghanistan, famous king Siladitya (589–647) of India, Nalanda Vihara (today Barragon Village in Bihar, India), the ancient Buddhism academic center of India and so on. The literature offers important information for people to study Middle Asia and South Asia before the 7th century. Without it, people can hardly research ancient India.

实善良、为求取佛经而不惧困难的一面，但人们更多地看到的是一个软弱无能、迂腐糊涂的佛教徒形象。通过《西游记》以及由这部小说改编的图画书、电影、电视等媒介，唐僧的文学形象和取经故事已为世人所熟知。

然而唐僧并非一个完全虚构的人物。唐僧的意思是来自唐帝国的僧人，历史上的唐僧，就是唐朝（618—907）佛教高僧玄奘（602—664）。他是7世纪时伟大的旅行家、翻译家和佛学家。在近1400年前，他不畏艰险，凭借坚定的信念、顽强的意志和杰出的智慧，跋涉数万公里，历时17年，远赴印度取经，创造了一个奇迹。

玄奘西行取经的过程，也是一次伟大的文化之旅。他回中国后写成了历史地理名著《大唐西域记》，记载他亲历的

玄奘法师像
Xuanzang.

Xuanzang was also a great translator. In the last 20 years of his life, he translated independently or took charge of translation of more than 1,300 volumes of Buddhist sutras. It was a hard work because he translated the Sanskrit, which is complex and difficult to learn, and then translate into Chinese. If compared to today's book size, the translated works can be converted into more than 400 books. It was really amazing. What's more, he also translated China's outstanding philosophic work *Tao Te Ching* and the Buddhist works in Chinese language into Sanskrit.

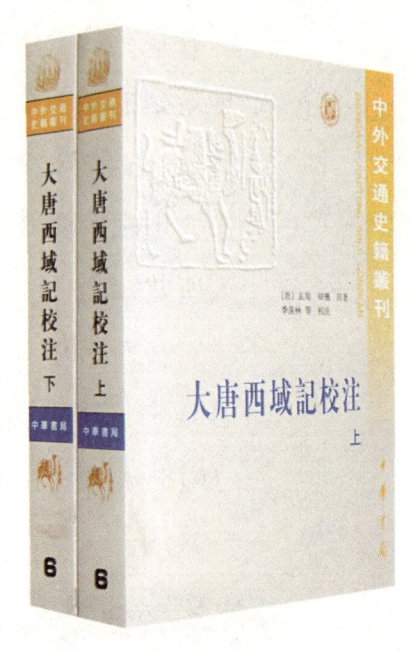

现代学者整理的《大唐西域记》
On Yuan Chwang's Travels in India, sorted by modern scolars.

Xuanzang made great contribution to the foreign-Chinese culture exchange and has been praised highly. In India there are pictures of him in the museums carrying his luggage to retrieve the Buddhist sutras and he is considered "sage" there. In the early 20th century, Vincent Smith, British scholar of India history, said, "Such a work—*On Yuan Chwang's Travels in India*—can never be overvalued." An Indian historian said that without the works of Xuanzang and the other Chinese scholars, "It is impossible to reproduce India's history."

110个和听别人讲述的28个城邦、地区、国家的地理、历史、风俗、物产、宗教、文化、政治等各方面的情况，其中提到了著名的阿富汗巴米扬大佛、印度历史上有名的国王戒日王（589—647）、印度古代佛教学术中心那烂陀寺（现在印度比哈尔邦的巴拉贡村）等。这部著作是人们了解7世纪前中亚、南亚历史的重要资料。如果不引用这部著作，人们几乎无法研究印度古代问题。

玄奘还是伟大的翻译家，他在生命的最后将近20年中，独自翻译或者主持翻译了佛教经典达1300余卷。这项工作非常艰苦，因为他是将极其复杂、难以掌握的梵文翻译成中文，而且译文质量很高。以现在的图书规模计算，他的这些翻译作品大约有400册之多。这是非常惊人的。而且，他还将中国卓越的哲学著作《道德经》和用汉语写成的佛学著作翻译成梵文。

玄奘为中外文化文流作出了重大贡献，因此获得了极高的评价。如今，印度的博物馆里陈列有他背着行李求取佛经的图像，把他当作"圣人"。20世纪初，研究印度历史的英国学者史密斯认为，"对这一部著作（指《大唐西域记》）无论评价多高也不会过

Xuanzang obtaining the Buddhist sutras from India was a blast in China then. After his death, the Buddhist disciples wrote many biographies for him, including the long biography (more than 80,000 Chinese characters) written by two of his students. These works have combined Xuanzang's stories with some Buddhist tales. Since then Xuanzang's Journey to West was apotheosized gradually and finally the fiction *the Journey to West* was completed.

The stories of Xuanzang about his pilgrimage introduced below were based on the historical records. Xuanzang was really a legend, given the true stories about his travels to Xinjiang, Middle Asia and India. They were not magic, as described in the fiction, but definitely had unique charm.

分"。一位印度历史学家则说，如果没有玄奘等中国人的著作，"重建印度史是完全不可能的"。

玄奘到印度取经、载誉归来的事迹，也在中国引起轰动。他去世后，佛教徒们为他写了多种传记，包括由他的两个学生所写的8万多字的长篇传记。在这些著作中，已经将玄奘的事迹与一些佛教神话故事结合起来。此后，人们就不断将唐僧西天取经的故事神化，最终形成了小说《西游记》。

下面介绍的玄奘西天取经故事，依据的是有关的历史记载。玄奘的一生的确很不平凡，尤其是他游历新疆、中亚、印度一带的真实故事，虽然不像小说所描写的那样神奇，却也别具魅力。

II

Earlier Experience of Xuanzang

In *the Journey to West*, Xuanzang's parents experienced many miseries, forcing Xuanzang to live in the temple since he was a baby. Of course it was just a folk story. As a matter of fact Xuanzang lived with his parents when he was a child.

Xuanzang was born in today's Yanshi City, Henan Province. He was named Chen Yi before he became a monk. According to the rule, one had to replace his lay name with a monastic name after becoming a monk. Xuanzang was his monastic name. His father, handsome and lettered, guided Xuanzang to study the Confucian classics. Xuanzang was very clever and could understand the meaning of the Confucian classics immediately, after his father told him once. He abode by them strictly. His father was very happy about his clever child, and his relatives and friends believed Xuanzang was a prodigy.

Though the youngest son of the family, Xuanzang was cautious and tender and cared for his parents. He was a

2

玄奘的早期经历

小说《西游记》中，玄奘的父母经历了短暂的辉煌和随后十分悲惨的遭遇，致使玄奘从婴儿时期开始就被迫生活在寺院中。当然这只是民间传说。事实上，玄奘小时候是跟父母生活在一起的。

玄奘的家乡是现在的河南省偃师市，他本来姓陈，名祎。按照规定，出家成为佛教徒之后要放弃原来的名字，另外取一个法号，玄奘就是他的法号。他的父亲是个相貌堂堂的美男子，很有文化修养，从小就指导玄奘学习儒家著作。玄奘非常聪明，听到父亲讲儒家经书里面的训诫，马上就能领会其意思，并严格执行。父亲很高兴，亲戚朋友也都认为玄奘是个神童。

玄奘是父亲最小的儿子，性格却很谨慎温和，懂得照顾父母。他是个非常早熟的孩子，喜欢研读严肃

very precocious child and loved studying serious books. He never played with the other children or joined in the fun if there was something interesting in the streets.

Why did Xuanzang finally became a monk since he received the Confucian education since he was a child? On the one hand, it was because he lost his dependence after his parents died when he was about 10 years old. On the other hand, his second eldest brother Changjie had become a monk in Luoyang (today in Henan Province). Changjie believed his intelligent brother would become an outstanding Buddhist scholar and took him to the temple.

At that time, a monk could be exempted from the duties of military service and taxes and get a certain area of land. Therefore the number of monks was strictly controlled. Emperor Yangdi of Sui Dynasty (569–618) sent an official named Zheng Shanguo to Luoyang to choose 14 persons as monks. There were several hundreds of candidates. Xuanzang did not take part in the selection because of young age and he watched the selection while standing by the door. Zheng Shanguo noticed the extraordinary child and asked him if he would like to be a monk. Xuanzang said yes. Then Zheng asked him the reason. Xuanzang replied, "I want to carry on the indoctrination of Buddha and enhance development of Buddhism." Zheng confirmed his ambition and admitted him, breaking the age rule. Zheng told his colleagues, "The child possesses

的书籍,从来不与别的孩子一起玩耍,街上有什么热闹的场面,他也从不出门去看。

　　既然从小接受儒家教育,那么玄奘为什么最终走上了学佛的道路呢?一方面,可能因为在他10岁左右时,父母已双双去世,他失去了依靠;另一方面,因为他的第二个哥哥长捷已经在洛阳(在现在的河南

河南洛阳奉先寺佛像
Buddhist statues in Fengxian Temple, Luoyang, Henan Province.

god-given bearing and must grow into the great one of Buddhism. What's a pity we cannot see in person how he realizes his ambition."

Xuanzang studied very hard after becoming a monk. He loved Mahayana and remembered all the content after studied the sutras only two times. He amazed all of his companions and was asked to repeat the master's lecture. His lecture was detailed and vivid, not inferior to his master's at all. He was 13 years old then and started to establish his belief in Mahayana.

After the founder of Buddhism Sakyamuni, there were different understandings and interpretations to the Buddhist tenets, and different schools were formed, mainly Mahayana and Hinayana. The Mahayana was a school started later, with the beliefs that Buddhism could help all to become Buddha and enter into the Elysium. The school was innovative comparatively. By contrast the earlier school, which was relatively conservative and emphasized individual cultivation, was named Hinayana. These two schools spread to China successively and generated different branches, which were in discord with each other.

Xuanzang favored Mahayana, but the translations and introduction to Mahayana were not rich in China. The translated scriptures were poor with lots of contradictions and mistakes. Xuanzang was confused by some Buddhist

省）一座寺院里做了僧人。长捷认为聪颖的弟弟能够成为优秀的佛学人才，就把他带到寺院里学习。

当时出家为僧可以享受不服兵役、不交税、并分配给一定数量的田地等优越条件，所以僧人的数量受到严格控制。隋炀帝（569—618）派一位叫郑善果的官员到洛阳来选拔14个人为僧，候选的有好几百人。玄奘因为年纪小，没有参加选拔，站在门边观看。郑善果注意到了这个气度不凡的小孩，就问他想不想出家。玄奘给了肯定的回答。郑善果又问他，出家为了什么？玄奘答道："我想继承佛祖如来的教导，发扬光大佛教。"郑善果非常赞赏他这种远大志向，就将他破格录取，并告诉同事："这个孩子的气质非常难得，将来一定是佛门中的伟大人才，可惜我们来不及亲眼看见他展翅腾飞的样子了。"

玄奘出家以后勤奋学习，有一位法师讲说一部大乘佛教的经书，他十分喜爱，学习了两遍，就全部记住了。大家都很惊异，让他到讲席上去复述一遍，结果他讲得详尽生动，与老师没有差别。这一年他13岁，开始确立对大乘学说的信仰。

佛教创始人释迦牟尼逝世后，佛教内部由于对

questions and wished to get guidance from more famous masters.

At that time Tang overthrew the Sui Dynasty (581–618) and Luoyang was hit by serious chaos caused by war. Xuanzang discussed with his brother to come to Chang'an (Xi'an, Shaanxi Province), the capital of the newly established Tang Dynasty. However, Chang'an was not in peace then and the brothers fled to Chengdu, Sichuan. Sichuan was relatively stable then and many famous monks came there. They set up many temples and debated with each other on the doctrines. Xunzang listened to sermons and studied hard. Several years later, his knowledge, experience and grace excelled among the others and he developed a widespread reputation.

After living five years in Chengdu, Xuanzang decided to go to Chang'an again. His brother Changjie wanted to stay in Chengdu and insisted Xuanzang stay too. Xuanzang wanted to pursue a wider Buddhist world and left his brother secretly. Accompanying the merchants, he crossed the beautiful Three Gorges, Jingzhou (Hubei Province), Xiangzhou (Anyang, Henan Province) and arrived in Chang'an again. On the trip he visited many famous masters.

After coming to Chang'an, he studied *Abhidharmakosa-sastra* following Master Yue. Bright and talented, he

教义有不同的理解和阐发,形成了许多派别,大致可归为大乘和小乘两大派别。大乘是晚起的派别,认为可以帮助所有人都成佛,进入极乐世界。这个教派具有一定革新性,而相对保守、强调个人修行的早期佛教派别就被称为小乘佛教。这两派学说先后传到中国,产生了许多支派,互相争执。

玄奘喜欢大乘学说,可是当时中国对佛经的翻译和介绍还不够丰富,译文也有许多问题,里面充满了矛盾和错误。玄奘对一些佛学问题感到疑惑,希望得

《涅槃图》,表现佛祖辞世的情景。明吴彬绘。
Painting of Nirvana, describing the scene that Sakyamuni passed away. Painted by Wu Bin, Ming Dynasty.

could understand the meaning after only listening once. Nobody could compare with him on the indepth study and interpretation of the hidden meaning. At that time two dignitaries named Fachang and Sengbian were in Chang'an, who were versed in Mahayana and Hinayana and famous Buddhist masters in the country. Many came to their lectures on Mahayana. Xuanzang made intensive discussion with them after listening to the lectures. The dignitaries were amazed by Xuanzang and said he was the swift horse of the Buddhist scholars, meaning he possessed extraordinary intelligence to make great achievements.

The more he learned, the more Xuanzang felt the Mahayana theory could not satisfy him. With increasing Buddhist knowledge, he found that there were many problems in the Buddhist sutras translated before. To solve the problems, he decided to go to India, the origin of Buddhism, to seek the Sanskrit sutras and make a thorough study.

At that time, a Buddhist monk came to China by sea from Middle India and lived in Chang'an. The monk was a disciple of Shilabhadra (about 528–651), authoritative Buddhist scholar of India and dignitary of Nalanda Vihara. Xuanzang consulted with him about the condition of Buddhism in India. He could not help but wish to go to India when he learned

到更多名师的指点。

这时，恰逢唐朝推翻隋朝（581—618）统治，洛阳一带经受了严重战乱。玄奘便和哥哥商议，前往新建立的唐王朝的首都长安（现在的陕西省西安市）。两人离开洛阳，到了长安。可是这时候的长安还没有安定下来，于是兄弟两人又跑到四川的成都。四川当时局势比较稳定，很多有名的僧人都聚集到成都，开设了很多寺院，互相论辩。玄奘来到这里，到处去听人讲经，勤学苦思。几年下来，他的学问、见识和风度就超出了其他僧人，名声传播到了很远的地方。

在成都住了五年之后，玄奘决定再回到长安。他哥哥长捷希望继续留在成都，并且坚持让弟弟也留下。但是玄奘想追求更广大的佛法世界。他偷偷离开哥哥，与商人结伴，穿过风光奇丽的三峡，一路经过荆州（在现在的湖北省）、相州（现在河南省的安阳市）等地，又来到了长安城。这一路上，他访问了诸多名师。

到长安城后，他跟着有名的岳法师学习《俱舍论》。他天资聪颖，听一遍就能够了解大意；至于深入探讨、阐发微妙的意义，更是没有人比得上他。这

Chang'an, Capital of Tang Dynasty

It is Xi'an City, Shaanxi Province. Chang'an was a capital city with the largest number of dynasties establishing their capital there, the longest time as a capital and the greatest influence in China with a great reputation in the world civilization history. It was the capital of the West Han Dynasty (206 BC–AD 25), the starting point of the famous Silk Road. In the peak time of Tang Dynasty, Chang'an was the largest and the most flourishing city in the world, covering 84 square kilometers, seven times the size of ancient Rome. The population reached one million, including many foreign merchants, emissaries and international students.

that Shilabhadra was familiar with theories of different Buddhist schools, especially the Mahayana classics *Yogacara-bhumi-sastra*. This strengthened his determination to go west for the sutras.

After making up his mind, Xuanzang contacted some companions wishing to go to India. They submitted the application to the government asking for permission for their journey to the west. In the fiction *the Journey to West*, Tangseng received encouragement and support from Li Shimin (599–649), Emperor Taizong of Tang Dynasty. But the truth is that the emperor did not approve their application and they could not get a Guosuo (similar to a passport). His companions gave up. Xuanzang was dead

唐都长安

位于现在陕西省西安市，是中国历史上建都朝代最多、时间最长、影响力最大的都城，在世界文明史上享有盛名。它也曾经是西汉（公元前206—公元25）王朝的首都，是著名的"丝绸之路"的起点。在盛唐时期，长安是当时规模最大、最繁华的国际都市，面积约84平方公里，相当于七个古代罗马城；人口达到百万，其中包括许多外国商人、使者、留学生等。

时长安有法常、僧辩两位高僧，精通大小乘，是全国知名的佛学大师。他们讲解大乘佛法，听讲的人非常多。玄奘认真地听了之后，跟他们进行深入讨论。这两位高僧都感叹说，玄奘是佛教学者中的千里马，意思是他拥有非凡的资质，可以取得非凡的成就。

可是越是深入学习，玄奘越觉得当时中国国内所讲的大乘理论不能令他满意；他的佛学知识日益广博，认为旧译的佛经有很多问题。怎么解决这个问题呢？他决定亲自前往佛教的发源地印度，求取梵文真经，进行彻底的研究。

恰好在这个时候，有一位中印度的佛教僧人从海

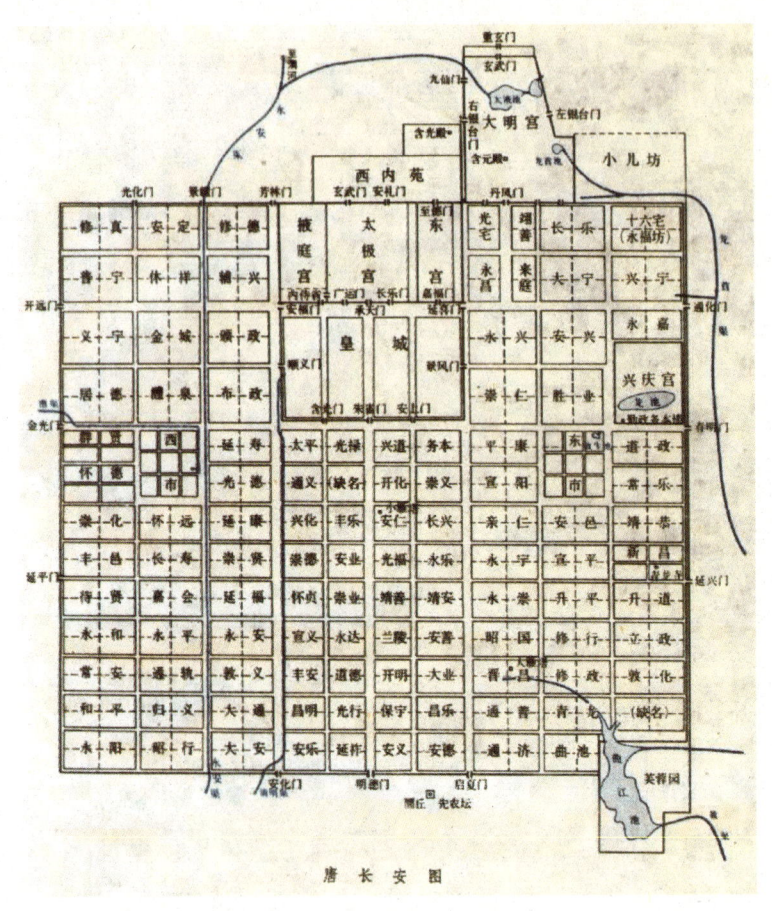

唐代长安城图
Painting of Chang'an City, Tang Dynasty.

set on his wish and decided to go to India alone to seek the essence of Buddhism there.

He was preparing secretly for the coming long and tough journey. First he started to learn Sanskrit. Secondly, he started to strengthen his physical condition in

路来到中国，住在长安。这位僧人是印度权威的佛学学者、那烂陀寺的高僧戒贤（约528—651）法师的学生，学问很渊博。玄奘诚恳地向他请教，了解印度当时佛学的情况。得知戒贤法师熟悉佛学各派理论，尤其精通大乘佛学经典《瑜伽师地论》，玄奘不禁悠然神往。这更坚定了他去西天取经的决心。

玄奘打定主意，就积极联系一些同伴，希望结伴前往印度。他们向政府递交了申请文书，请求政府准许他们前往西天。在小说《西游记》中，唐僧得到唐太宗李世民（599—649）的鼓励和赞助前往西天。但历史上的真实情况是，皇帝没有批准玄奘等人的申请，这样他们就无法获得"过所"（类似于现在的护照）。同伴都放弃了原来的想法，只有玄奘非常坚决，决定独自到遥远的印度去探求佛学的真谛。

他悄悄地为将来的艰苦旅程作准备。首先，他开始找老师学习梵文。其次，考虑到西行之路的艰险，他开始有意识地加强体

唐太宗李世民
Emperor Taizong Li Shimin, Tang Dynasty.

Li Shimin, Emperor Taizong of Tang Dynasty

The second emperor of the Tang Dynasty, famous enlightened emperor and politician in China's history. During his reign, he developed a vigorous economy and attached importance to people's life. The country was flourishing with a stable society, incorruptible government and people who were well-off. The title of his reign was Zhenguan, thus the period was named Golden Years of Zhenguan, marked by peace, prosperity, openness and efficient government.

preparation for the hardship of the upcoming journey. He quietly waited for the right opportunity.

In the year when he was 26 years old, or the fall of the first year of Zhenguan (627) under the reign of Emperor Taizong of Tang Dynasty, the Emperor ordered the evacuation of the population in Chang'an to the other areas due to the worry of an insufficient food supply in Chang'an caused by frost. Xuanzang took this chance to leave Chang'an and started his journey to the west.

> **唐太宗李世民**
>
> 唐朝第二位皇帝，中国历史上著名的开明帝王和政治家。他在统治期间，大力发展经济，重视民生，唐朝社会安定，政治清明，人民生活富裕安康，出现了很繁荣的景象。他在位时年号为贞观，所以人们把这段时期称为"贞观之治"。

力锻炼。他不动声色地等待合适的机会。

在他26岁那年，即唐太宗贞观元年（627）的秋天，唐太宗担心遭到霜灾的长安粮食不够吃，下令准许首都的人口分散到其他地方。玄奘趁机离开长安，踏上了前往西天的道路。

III

Stealthily Cross the Border for Buddhist Scriptures

Xuanzang left Chang'an along with a monk from Qinzhou (Tianshui, Gansu Province). After spending a night in Qinzhou, he came to Lanzhou (in Gansu Province) along with the others and then to Liangzhou (Wuwei City, Gansu Province).

Liangzhou was an important city of west China and the necessary road connecting the east and the west with many merchants coming from different countries. Xuanzang was a famous monk at that time. He lived there for a month giving lectures on scriptures for the local monks and common people. The foreign merchants came to his lectures and spread the word after returning back that Xuanzang from Great Tang would go to India for the Buddhist sutras.

The news flew to Li Daliang, the local governor of Liangzhou. At that time the Tang Empire was new and the regime was not stable. The northwest border area was often attacked by west Turks tribes. Therefore

3

偷渡国境的取经人

唐三彩骆驼商俑
Tang tri-color camel pottery.

　　玄奘离开长安时，与一个来自秦州(现在甘肃省的天水市)的僧人结伴同行。到秦州住了一个晚上，又与人结伴前往兰州（在现在的甘肃省），然后来到凉州（现在甘肃省的武威市）。

　　凉州是当时中国西部地区的一个重要城市，是东西方交通的要道，许多国家的商人往来不断。玄奘已经是有名的僧人，他在这儿住了一个多月，为当地的僧人和一般民众讲经。各国商人也都来听讲。这些人回到各自的国家以后，都报告他们的首领

the central government ordered to block the border to prevent anybody leaving the country without permission. Li Daliang took strict measures. When he learned that a monk from Chang'an was planning to go abroad, he worried Xuanzang had other purposes and sent somebody to ask Xuanzang about his purpose. Xuanzang replied he decided to go to India for the Buddhist sutras. Li Daliang ordered him to return Chang'an. Fortunately a Buddhist leader there valued Xuanzang highly and supported his ambition. He sent two disciples secretly to escort Xuanzang to go westwards. To avoid being hunted by the government, they had to hide in the daylight and hurry on with their journey in the night until they arrived in Guazhou (in Gansu Province).

At that time, Guazhou was almost the most western town of the Tang Dynasty. The local governor revered Buddhism and received Xuanzang warmly. But the governor did not know of Xuanzang's plan to go to the west. He lived in Guazhou temporally and inquired about the way to the west. He was told that there was a torrential river (River Shule) more than 50 *li* (25 km) to the north. By the river was the famous Yumen Pass (near Dunhuan, Gansu Province). Crossing the pass one would see the desert. There were five beacon towers stationed by Tang's soldiers to prevent illegal border crossings. Following the five towers was a large desert named Moheyanqi,

说，大唐的玄奘法师将要到印度去取经求法。

这个消息也传到了凉州地方长官李大亮的耳朵里。当时唐帝国刚刚建立，政权尚未完全巩固，西北一带边境又常常遭受西突厥部落的威胁，所以中央政府下令封锁边境，不准人民私自出国。李大亮防范很严。他听说有一个从长安来的僧人要到外国去，担心玄奘有别的用意，就派人去问玄奘。玄奘回答说，要上西天取经。李大亮命令他返回长安。幸好，当地有

敦煌莫高窟第296窟壁画，描绘"丝绸之路"上商人们的旅途生活。
Fresco of No. 296 Grotto, Dunhuang Mogao Grottos, describing the travel of businessmen on the Silk Road.

which was more than 800 *li* (400 km) wide. After crossing the desert one would arrive in Yiwu Kingdom (Hami, Xinjiang), which was controlled by the West Turks instead of Tang. In the early years of the Tang Dynasty, Turks were strong and controlled the whole Middle Asia west to Yumen Pass. Turks was a nomad people and the Turkish cavalry was a great threat to travelers.

Xuanzang was anxious when he learned of the difficulties of the journey ahead. Unfortunately his horse died from illness. He stayed in Guazhou for more than

玉门关遗址，甘肃敦煌
Site of Yumen Pass, Dunhuang, Gansu.

一位佛教领袖，很器重玄奘，对他取经的理想也很支持和同情，就秘密派了两个徒弟送玄奘向西走。为了躲过官方的追查，他们不敢公然上路，只能白天躲起来，晚上赶路，就这样到了瓜州(在现在的甘肃省)。

在当时，瓜州差不多已经是唐朝最西面的城镇了。当地的地方长官敬重佛法，热情招待玄奘，但并不知道他要到西天去。玄奘在瓜州暂时住下来，向人打听西行路线。有人告诉他，北边50多里（一里相当于约0.5公里）有一条水流很急的河（现在叫疏勒河），河上就是有名的玉门关（在现在甘肃省的敦煌市附近），出了这个关口，就是沙漠。沙漠中有五座烽火台，上面都驻扎着唐朝的士兵，防止人们偷越国境。五烽之外，是一个叫莫贺延碛的大沙漠，宽800多里。过了莫贺延碛，就到伊吾国（现在新疆的哈密市）了，那里还不是唐的领土，由西突厥控制。唐朝初年，突厥的势力十分强大，控制着玉门关以西的整个中亚地方。突厥是一个游牧民族，对于旅客来说，突厥骑兵是一种巨大的威胁。

玄奘听到道路这样艰险难行，非常发愁。不幸的是，他的马也病死了。他就在瓜州耽搁了一个多月。就

a month. Just at that time Li Daliang discovered that Xuanzang did not return Chang'an but traveled west. He issued a "wanted" circular to hunt for Xuanzang.

A local official in Guazhou named Li Chang who was a devoted Buddhist wanted to help Xuanzang. He asked, "Are you the person in the wanted circular?" Xuanzang did not know how to reply. Li Chang said, "Please tell me the truth and I would work out some solution for you." When Xuanzang told him the truth, Li Chang tore the circular and told Xuanzang, "You must start immediately."

Xuanzang bought a horse immediately and prepared to leave. However, he was troubled because he did not have a guide. One day a strong man from the West Region (a collective name to the Middle Asia, Western Asia and Indian Peninsula) came to the temple where Xuanzang lived to worship Buddha. The man named Shi Pantuo and Xuanzang held the ceremony accepting him as a Buddhist after talking with him. Shi agreed to escort Xuanzang to cross the five beacon towers.

They arranged to meet each other at dusk the next day. Shi Pantuo brought an old man of the west region who had come to Yiwu Kingdom more than 30 times. The old man advised Xuanzang not to go because he would probably die in the journey. Xuanzang said decisively, "I swear I will go to the west for the gospel. If I cannot reach India, I would never return to the east and I will not regret

在这时，凉州的李大亮发现玄奘并没有回长安，而是偷偷跑到西边来了，就发下通缉令，要求各地捕捉玄奘。

瓜州一个叫李昌的地方官员拿到通缉令，就来找玄奘。李昌是虔诚的佛教徒，想帮助玄奘。他问："您是不是文书中所说的这个人？"玄奘不知道怎么回答。李昌说："您请说实话吧，我一定为您想办法。"玄奘便告诉了他实情。李昌将文书撕毁，对玄奘说："您应该赶快动身。"

玄奘赶紧买了一匹马，准备动身，但苦于没有向导。他住在当地的寺院里，这一天忽然来了一个强壮的西域人拜佛。这个西域人叫石槃陀，西域是当时中国人对西边的中亚、西亚、印度半岛等地的统称。两人进行交谈，玄奘为他举行仪式，接受他为佛教徒，而他答应送玄奘走过五座烽火台。

两人约好第二天黄昏见面。石槃陀带来一位西域老人。这个老人曾到过伊吾国30多次，劝玄奘不要前进，以免牺牲了性命。玄奘非常坚决地说："我为了寻求真理，发誓到西天。如果到不了印度，决不东归，就算死在途中也决不后悔。"老人见劝不退他，就提议将自己的一匹老马换给玄奘，因为这匹马曾15

even if I die in the journey." Seeing Xuanzang's resolve, the old man suggested replacing Xuanzang's horse with his old horse because it had been to Yiwu Kingdom for 15 times. Thus they exchanged the horses.

Xuanzang and Shi Pantuo started in the night and came to the upper reaches of the river outside of Yumen Pass. Shi Pantuo built a bridge by chopping down a tree and they crossed the river. It was midnight and both of them fell into sleep. Worried that he would be punished by the government because he helped Xuanzang cross the border illegally, Shi Pantuo took out his knife in the midnight to Xuanzang. Xuanzang sit up vigilantly and read aloud the scripture. Shi Pantuo came back and slept. After they walked for a while the next day, Shi Pantuo told Xuanzang finally he wanted to go home because he greatly feared being involved. Xuanzang swore that he would never implicate him if the government caught them. After sending Shi Pantuo a horse, Xuanzang let him leave. So Xuanzang had to try to cross the border by himself.

In the desert alone, Xuanzang had to confirm the direction by the bones and horse manure. He saw a mirage in the desert showing several hundreds of cavalries with banners and weapons. The mirage was very clear from a long distance but disappeared when he got closer. Xuanzang thought at first they were robbers and then demon and monsters. He could not explain the

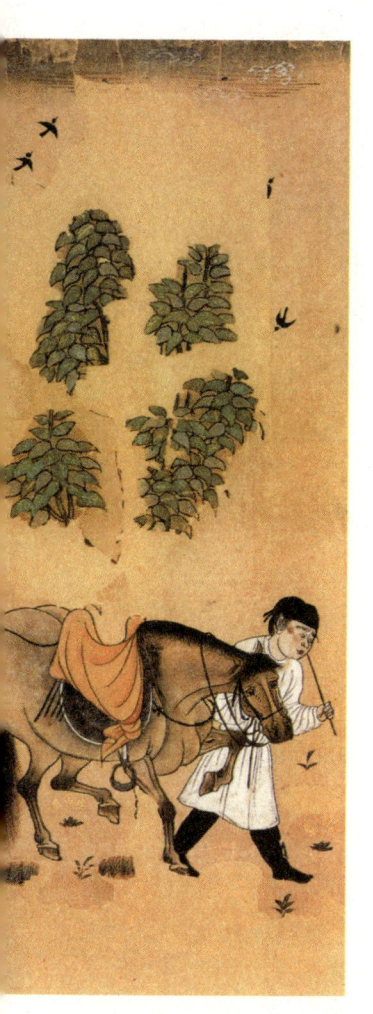

新疆吐鲁番出土的《侍马图》绢画，表现了西域人与骏马的形象。
Silk painting of Grooms and Horses unearthed in Turpan, Xinjiang, reflecting the image of west region people and horses.

次往返于伊吾国，认识道路。于是两人就换了马。

玄奘和石槃陀在夜里出发，来到玉门关外河流的上游。石槃陀砍下树木搭成一座桥，两人就这样过了河。这时已经是深夜，两人各自睡下。石槃陀可能是担心帮助玄奘偷越国境会受到官府严厉处罚，半夜突然拔刀而起，走向玄奘；玄奘警觉地坐起来，念诵佛经。石槃陀于是又回去睡觉。第二天天亮，两人走了一段路，石槃陀终于提出，害怕受到连累，想回家去。玄奘向他发誓，如果被捉住，即使粉身碎骨也不会牵连到他，又送了他一匹马，让石槃陀走了。这样，玄奘仍然要靠自己的力量尝试偷越国境。

玄奘独自走进沙漠，只能靠白骨、马粪来确认前进的方向。在这里，他遭遇了沙漠中的海市蜃楼，忽然看见有几百名骑兵，拿着旌旗、武器，满布在沙漠间；远看非常清楚，靠近时就渐渐消

玄奘西行求法壁画，陕西榆林石窟第3窟
Fresco of Xuanzang's Journey to West for Buddhist Scriptures, No.3 Grotto, Yulin Stone Grotto, Shaanxi Province.

phenomena in a scientific way at that time and had to overcome his fear with a strong will.

After coming near the first beacon tower, he hid in the sand ditch until the night and walked to the tower secretly for drinking water and replenishing the water bag. Suddenly two arrows flew toward him and nearly hit his leg. He knew he was discovered and shouted loudly to the soldiers to stop shooting. He came to the beacon tower with his horse and the soldiers took him to the officer defending the turret.

When Wang Xiang, the officer, confirmed the monk was Xuanzang on the wanted circular, he suggested Xuanzang go back to his hometown Dunhuang (in Gansu

失了。玄奘起初以为是强盗，后来又以为是妖魔鬼怪；在当时的条件下，他不能科学地解释这种现象，只能凭着坚定的意志来战胜恐惧的情绪。

他来到第一座烽火台附近，躲在沙沟里面，等到晚上才偷偷走近烽火台。那里有水源，他去喝水和用皮袋子取水。这时忽然飞来两箭，几乎射中他的膝部。他知道被发现了，于是大声叫喊，让守兵停止射箭。他牵着马走近烽火台，士兵们带他去见负责防守这座烽火台的军官。

这位军官名叫王祥。当他确认眼前的僧人正是凉州通缉令上的玄奘时，他提出了一个建议，说西天太

烽火台遗迹，甘肃敦煌附近
Site of beacon tower, near Dunhuang, Gansu.

烽火台遗迹，新疆克孜尔尕哈
Site of beacon tower, Kizil Gaha, Xinjiang.

Province), where the people would receive Xuanzang warmly. Xuanzang insisted on his plan and explained that he had been recognized by the dignitaries in Luoyang and Chang'an. He had become famous in Luoyang and Chang'an and did not need to go to Dunhuang. He said he was sorry that the scriptures he saw and heard were not complete. That was the reason he planned to the west against the difficulties and risks. He told Wang Xiang he would not return whatever happened.

Wang Xiang was moved by Xuanzang and asked him to have a rest first. The next morning, Wang Xiang prepared food and water for Xuanzang and saw him off in person. Wang told Xuanzang about a shortcut to save more than 200 *li* (100 km) to the fourth beacon tower directly. He told Xuanzang, "The officer in charge there is a good man. You

远了，玄奘恐怕不能到达，不如到他的家乡敦煌（在现在的甘肃省）去，那里的人们一定很欢迎玄奘。玄奘坚持自己的想法，他解释说，自己在洛阳和长安都已得到佛教高僧们的认可，也算是小有名气的人物了；如果仅仅是为了追求自己的名声，留在长安或洛阳就可以了，又何必要去敦煌？因为所闻所见的教义还有不周全的地方，他的内心仍然感到遗憾，所以才不怕丧失性命、不畏艰难危险前往西天寻求佛法。他向王祥表示，无论如何都不会回头向东移动一步。

　　王祥被他打动，请他先休息。第二天早晨，王祥

新疆罗布泊雅丹地貌
Yadan landform of Lop Nur, Xinjiang.

> ### Dunhuang
>
> Dunhuang is a city in the intersection of Gansu, Qinghai and Xinjiang and under the administration of Gansu. In the early years of the Tang Dynasty, Buddhism was very popular there and was the Buddhist center of Hexi (the area of Gansu and Qinghai west to the Yellow River). Dunhuang is famous for the grotto Buddhist arts and ancient literatures. There are Mogao Grotto, Yulin Grotto and West Qianfo Grotto and so on.

just tell him I asked you to come to him and he will help you." Xuanzang appreciated Wang's help very much and parted him in tears.

At the fourth beacon tower, Xuanzang had a similar experience and was nearly shot by the guards. When he mentioned the name of Wang Xiang, he was received warmly. The officer there presented Xuanzang a large leather water bag, horses and food and told him the way to avoid the fifth beacon tower.

With the help of the two officers, Xuanzang finally got away from the hunting of Tang's guards. However, the difficulties and dangers to the west had just started for him.

敦煌

位于现在中国甘肃、青海、新疆三省（区）交汇的地方，现在属于甘肃省。唐朝初年，这里社会生活稳定，佛教极为兴盛，是河西（现在甘肃、青海两省黄河以西的地区）地区的佛教中心。敦煌以石窟佛教艺术和古代文献闻名于世，现存莫高窟、榆林窟、西千佛洞等重要历史文化景观。

为玄奘准备好食物和水，亲自送他上路。王祥给玄奘指了一条近路，可以少走200多里路，直接到第四烽。他又对玄奘说："第四烽负责的军官也是个好人，你到那儿说，是我让您过去的。"玄奘非常感激，与王祥哭着分手了。

在第四座烽火台那儿，玄奘遭遇了同样的情形，差点被守兵的箭射中。但当他说出王祥的名字时，对方就很热情地接待他，送了他很大的装水用的皮袋子和马匹、食物，并告诉他绕过第五座烽火台的道路。

这样，在两位军官的帮助下，玄奘终于脱离了唐朝守兵的视线。但对他来说，西行的艰险才刚刚开始。

IV

Hardship and Dangers in the Journey to West

The journey to west was very long for Xuanzang. He had to cross the area controlled by Khan of the West Turks first, then Pamirs, and then cross the snow-covered mountain to India from today's Afghanistan through Middle Asian countries. The road he covered is what we call the Silk Road today. The Silk Road can be divided into the north, the central and the south routes. Xuanzang basically took the north and the central one. It was an untraversed road and he met numerous difficulties and dangers, sometimes inhospitable natural environments and sometimes unfriendly or complex human relations. In *the Journey to West*, Tangseng experienced 81 dangers before he arrived in India. In history Xuanzang experienced many dangers and difficulties too. Of course he also saw the customs of different countries, spread his Buddhist thinking and observed and recorded information of these countries in detail.

4
西行路上多艰险

玄奘西行之路非常漫长,他要先通过西突厥可汗的控制区,然后越过帕米尔高原,取道中亚各国,再从现在的阿富汗越过大雪山进入印度。他经过的道路,就是现在称为"丝绸之路"的道路。"丝绸之路"分为北、中、南三条线路,他基本上是沿着北线和中线行进。这条遥远的道路人迹罕至,他一路上所遇到的艰难和危险非常多,有的是恶劣的自然环境,有的则是不友善的或复杂的人际关系。《西游记》里说唐僧历经81次磨难才到达西天,其实历史上玄奘经历的磨难也很多。当然,在这个过程中,他也体验到了各国风情,传播了他的佛学思想,并细心观察和记录了各国的详细情况。

玄奘离开唐朝的边关后,进入了广阔无人的莫贺延碛沙漠。赶了100多里路,玄奘迷了路。他打算喝一

Silk Road

The Silk Road is the earliest channel of economic and cultural exchange between the east and the west. It started from Chang'an and extended to India and Europe after crossing the West Region. The silk, tea and iron wares of China were distributed to the west, and likewise, the technique, religion and customs of the west were introduced to China through the channel. The road is known as the Silk Road because ancient Romans loved silk. The Silk Road started very early and experienced two peak periods in the Han Dynasty (206 BC–AD 220) and Tang Dynasty respectively.

After leaving the border pass of Tang Dynasty, Xuanzang entered the endless and unpopulated Moheyanqi Desert. After covering more than 100 *li* (50 km) road, he got lost. Unfortunately he spilled the water bag when he was drinking water and lost all the water supply for next several days. These misfortunes shook Xuanzang's will and he wanted to go back to the beacon tower first. But after walking several miles, he remembered his oath and encouraged himself: I would rather die in the journey to the west than retreat to go on living. He changed the direction and kept forward towards the northwest.

The desert in the night is as splendid as the starry sky

丝绸之路

"丝绸之路"是东西方最早的经济、文化交流通道。它从中国古都长安开始,通过西域,伸展到印度和欧洲等地。中国的丝绸、茶叶、铁器等和各种技术通过这里传播到西方,而西方各国的工艺、宗教、风俗等也由这里传入中国。由于古罗马人对丝绸的热爱,这条道路被称为"丝绸之路"。"丝绸之路"的起源很早,汉(前206—公元220)、唐时期是它的两个兴盛期。

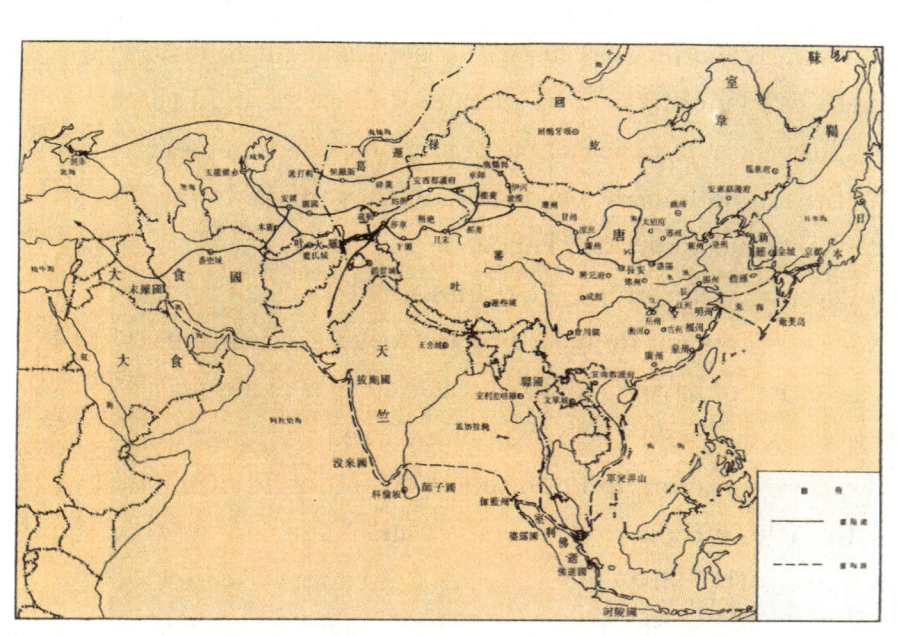

"丝绸之路"古地图
Ancient map of the Silk Road.

沙漠
Desert.

in the early morning because there is twinkling light that looks like lanterns held by demons. In fact the light is wildfire, the automatic flaming of phosphine decomposed by the rotting human remains or animal corpses. In the daylight sandstorm often happen in the desert. The sand rolled up by the strong wind flies in the sky like rain. Xuanzang was not frightened by the tough environment. However, not having a drop of water for four nights and five days, he could not sustain himself and lay down in the desert praying to Bodhisattva. At midnight of the fifth night, a cool wind blew over and Xuanzang was refreshed. The thirsty old horse stood up and walked for several miles to another road against Xuanzang's rein.

点水，但一不小心竟然将盛水的皮袋打翻，水马上渗入沙中不见了。够喝好几天的水就此丧失，又完全迷失了方向，玄奘一时动摇了，回转马头想先回到烽火台。但走了十几里，他想到自己发过的誓言，于是重新鼓励自己：宁可向西走而死，决不东归而生！他再度拨转马头，向西北方向前进。

大沙漠的晚上，黑暗中好像有很多妖魔鬼怪举着点亮的灯火，就像清晨的星空一样灿烂。这种火其实是磷火，即人或者动物的尸体腐烂时分解出的磷化氢自动燃烧的现象。白天常常会遇到沙尘暴，狂风卷起黄沙，像下雨一样漫天飞舞。环境如此恶劣，玄奘并没有畏惧，但一连四个晚上和五个白天，他没能喝到一滴水，最后实在支持不住，只能卧倒在沙漠中，向菩萨祷告。第五天半夜时分，忽然吹来一阵凉风，玄奘精神为之一振。那匹同样饥渴难当的老马也站起来，走了十几里路。老马不顾玄奘的拉扯走向另一条路，于是发现了青草和水源。玄奘和马在这儿休息了一整天，恢复了体力，带了足够的水和草继续上路。两天之后，他终于走出沙漠，到达伊吾国境。类似这样的危险和困难，在他的西行路上多得数不清。

Finally they found the green grass and a water source. Xuanzang and his horse stayed there for a whole day for refreshment and then continued their journey with sufficient water and fodder. Two days later, he walked out of the desert and reached the territory of Yiwu Kingdom. Xuanzang experienced numerous difficulties and dangers in the journey to west.

Yiwu Kingdom became a part of Empire Tang in the sixth year of Zhenguan Period (632). When Xuanzang arrived there, it was an independent kingdom. Xuanzang lodged in a temple where an old Chinese monk lived. When the monk learned Xuanzang came from China, he was so excited that he could not wait to dress properly and greeted Xuanzang barefooted. He hugged Xuanzang and cried, "I could not expect today that I could see my countryman again!" Xuanzang was moved deeply by the old monk. Upon the news, the king of Yiwu Kingdom came to visit Xuanzang too and invited him to the palace.

Xuanzang planned to go to the Khan palace of the West Turks directly from Yiwu Kingdom to get the passport from Turk to India. Unexpectedly, the envoy of King Qu Wentai of Gaochang Kingdom was in Yiwu Kingdom at the time and reported to Qu Wentai about Xuanzang. Gaochang Kingdom was affected by Chinese culture deeply and the whole country embraced Buddhism. Qu Wentai immediately sent an envoy to Yiwu Kingdom and

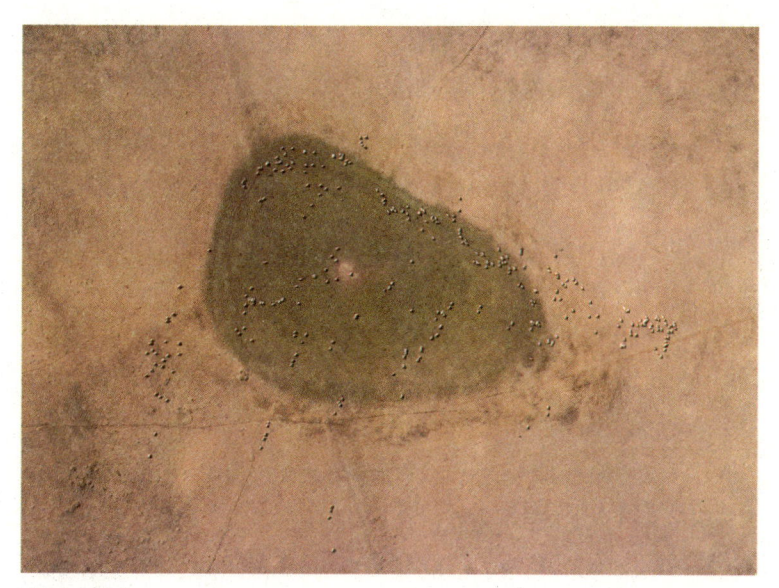

沙漠中的绿洲
Oasis in the desert.

伊吾国于唐太宗贞观六年(632)成为唐帝国的一部分,而玄奘到达的时候,它还是个独立的小国。玄奘投宿一所寺院,寺里有一位中国老僧,听说他来自中国,来不及穿好衣服,光着脚就跑出来迎接,抱着他痛哭说:"想不到今天还能够再次看见故乡来的人!"经历生死考验的玄奘听了,也深为感动。伊吾国王知道消息,也来拜访,并请玄奘到自己的宫里去做客,热情地招待他。

玄奘本想从这里直奔西突厥可汗的王廷所在地,

requested the King of Yiwu Kingdom to send Xuanzang to Gaochang.

Xuanzang came to Gaochang. It was midnight when he arrived in Gaochang's capital Jiaohe (west to Turpan, Xinjiang). The king received Xuanzang in person together with a number of attendants.

"When I heard your name, I was so happy that I forgot eating and sleeping because I was so looking forward to see you. My wife and I did not go to bed when we learned you would arrive tonight. We prayed to Buddha and wait here especially for you."

Early the next morning, the king had taken the queen and many others to pay respects to Xuanzang before he got up. He invited the dignitaries of the kingdom to visit Xuanzang, including an 80-year-old. The king asked the dignitary to persuade Xuanzang to stay in Gaochang and give up his plan to India. Xuanzang did not accept.

After a dozen of days, Xuanzang made his adieu to the king. The king tried to reason him again and again. Xuanzang said, "My journey to India is not for enshrinement or worship. I feel sad that China's Buddhist scriptures are not complete. Many of my puzzles cannot be solved. So I swear I will go to India for the Buddhist scripture so that the Chinese Buddhists could learn Mahayana. My will grows stronger and stronger and I cannot give it up halfway. I hope you abandon the idea

取得突厥可汗的护照前往印度。没有想到，这时高昌国王麹文泰的使臣正在伊吾国，遇见玄奘，回去报告国王。高昌国受汉族文化影响很深，并且全国上下都信奉佛教。麹文泰马上派遣使者赶到伊吾国，要求伊吾国王把玄奘送到高昌。

玄奘只得前往高昌。他到达高昌国的都城交河城（在现在新疆的吐鲁番以西）时已经是半夜。国王带了大量侍从亲自迎接，说："我自从听见法师的名字，高兴得忘记了吃饭和睡觉，天天盼着您来。知道您今晚会赶到，我和妻子都没有睡，诵经念佛，诚心等候。"

高昌都城交河故城
Ancient city of Jiaohe, capital of Gaochang.

of making me stay here." The king said, "My wish will not change what even the Congling Mountain can move. Please trust me for my sincerity." Congling Mountain was the collective name in ancient China to Pamirs, Kunlun Mountains and Karakorum Mountain. The king did his best to persuade Xuanzang to stay but Xuanzang refused. Finally the king was angry and threatened, "You may stay or I will send you back China. Please accept my suggestion." Xuanzang said the king could retain him physically, but not mentally.

Xuanzang fasted to show his resolution. On the fourth day the king gave up when when he found the monk was dying. He swore before Buddha that he would help Xuanzang go India for the Buddhist scripture. The king became the sworn brother of Xuanzang and gave two requirements: first Xuanzang should stay in Gaochang giving lectures on Buddhism for one month; second, after coming back from India, Xuanzang should live in Gaochang for three years and accept enshrinement and worship. Xuanzang agreed and started to take food. In the fiction *the Journey to West* there was the episode Emperor Taizong became sworn brothers of Xuanzang. In history it was Gaochang king.

When Xuanzang gave lectures on the Buddhist scriptures, the king and his mother and ministers came to the lectures in person. When Xuanzang was to step on the

第二天一早，玄奘尚未起床，国王已带了王妃和许多人前来请安。他请出国中的高僧陪伴玄奘，其中一位已年过八旬。国王让这位老僧劝玄奘住在高昌，不必再往西天，玄奘没有答应。

过了十几天，玄奘辞行。国王再三劝说，玄奘表示："我这次西行，不是为了接受供养。我感到痛心的是中国的佛法不够完备，心中有很多疑惑不能解决，所以发愿到西天取经，使中国信徒也能听到大乘佛法。这种心愿只可能一天比一天坚强，岂能半途而废？希望您不要再抱着留下我的想法。"国王说道："即使葱岭可以转动，我这种心愿也不会改变，请相信我的诚意。"葱岭是中国古代对帕米尔高原及昆仑山、喀喇昆仑山等西部诸山的统称。国王苦苦相劝，玄奘仍然不答应。国王最后生气了，威胁说："要么您留下，要么我把您送回中国去。请您还是接受我的建议吧。"玄奘表示，即使留下他的身体，也留不住他的心。

玄奘以绝食表示决心。到了第四天，国王见玄奘气息微弱，就向他表示忏悔，并请他一起到佛前发誓，愿意帮助他到印度取经。国王还与玄奘结拜为兄弟，并提出两个要求：一是在高昌讲经一个月，二是

platform, the king lowered his body and asked Xuanzang to use him as a step. It was a very high etiquette. When Xuanzang was to start his journey again, the king arranged four young monks to accompany him and prepared a large number of clothes, gloves and boots, and money, enough for 20 years of consumption. The king wrote letters to the kings on the way and sent his officials to escort Xuanzang to Khan of the West Turk. Xuanzang appreciated the king's help. The king accompanied Xuanzang for a long distance when the monk started his journey.

Now Xuanzang was not alone but with a team. They headed eastward and suddenly met a group of robbers when they nearly reached Yanqi Kingdom (Yanqi Hui

古国高昌遗迹
Relics of Gaochang.

从印度回来时在高昌住三年，接受供养。玄奘答应下来，这才恢复进食。小说《西游记》中有唐太宗与玄奘结拜为兄弟的情节，而历史上，与玄奘结为兄弟的是这位高昌国王。

  玄奘在高昌讲经时，国王的母亲、国王和大臣们都亲自前来听讲。玄奘将登上讲座时，国王就低身跪下让他踩着自己上去，这是一种高规格的礼节。等玄奘要上路时，国王为他安排了四个年轻僧人为伴，准备了大量服装、手套、靴子等物品，还有许多钱财，足够他在路上使用20年。国王给沿途各国君主写了亲

Autonomous County, Xinjiang). The robbers left after robbing some properties. Xuanzang and his companions stopped for a rest. Dozens of merchants wanted to rush down the road for their businesses and started secretly in the midnight. Unfortunately they were attacked and killed by the robbers. The next morning Xuanzang saw the tragedy and could do nothing but sigh. Yanqi Kingdom was once intruded by Gaochang and the king was unwilling to exchange the horses for Xuanzang. Xuanzang lived there only one night and left. However, careful Xuanzang still wrote down some information of the country.

Departing Yanqi Kingdom, Xuanzang headed west and entered Qiuci Kingdom (Kuqa County, Xinjiang) after crossing a river and several hundred miles. Qiuci was an important state on the Silk Road and the customs there were affected by India. The king, ministers and dignitaries embraced Xuanzang with a red-carpet ceremony. The local people set up tents, brought the important Buddhist statues and played music. Somebody presented Xuanzang a plate of fresh flowers and Xuanzang scattered the flowers before the Buddhist statues deferentially. The ceremony lasted for a long time and was not concluded before dark. The next day the king in person invited Xuanzang to the palace for a banquet. The local Hinayana did not abandon meat while it was forbid eating meat in Mahayana. Thus

笔信，并派官员护送玄奘前往西突厥可汗那里。玄奘十分感激。他上路的时候，国王送出很远。

现在玄奘已不是一个人，他带领着一支队伍。他们向西而行，快到焉耆国（现在新疆的焉耆回族自治县）时，突然遭遇一群强盗，这些强盗索取了一些财物后离去。玄奘等人停下来休息，而与他们同行的几十

柏孜克里克石窟，高昌时代的佛教石窟建筑，新疆吐鲁番
Bezkilik Grotto, Buddhist grotto building of Gaochang times, Turpan, Xinjiang.

the king arranged him to have a vegetarian diet.

At the welcoming ceremony, Xuanzang was arranged sitting next to the local authority of Buddhism Mokslagupta who had studied in India for more than 20 years and read many Buddhist scriptures, enjoying high prestige and social status in the kingdom. Xuanzang paid a visit to Mokslagupta who received Xuanzang with common etiquette and did not recognize his Buddhist culture. The old monk told Xuanzang arrogantly, "We have all the Buddhist scriptures here, enough for you to

龟兹故城遗址
Site of ancient city of Qiuci.

个商人想先赶去做生意，半夜私自出发，结果走了没多远就被强盗抢劫，几十人都被杀死。第二天早晨，玄奘一行经过，看到这种情形，只能叹息。他们到了焉耆，这个国家因为曾被高昌侵扰，不愿意帮助他们换马。玄奘等人住了一晚上就离开了，但细心的玄奘还是记录了这个国家的一些情况。

玄奘从焉耆国西行，渡过一条大河，走了700多里，进入龟兹国(现在新疆的库车县)。龟兹是当时"丝绸之路"上的重要国家，风俗习惯受到印度影响。龟兹的国王、大臣和一些高僧都来迎接玄奘，欢迎仪式很隆重。当地人搭起帐篷，把一些重要的佛像搬过来，奏起音乐。有人向玄奘献上一盘鲜花，玄奘端着这盘鲜花非常恭敬地到佛像前去散花。仪式进行了很长时间，到晚上才结束。第二天国王亲自来请玄奘进宫，宴席上有肉食，因为当地的小乘佛教并不戒绝肉食。而玄奘宗奉的大乘佛教规定是不吃肉食的，于是国王另外给他安排了素食。

在欢迎仪式上，玄奘被安排坐在当地的佛教权威木叉毱多之下。木叉毱多曾在印度学习20多年，读了很多佛经，在当地威望和地位很高。玄奘前去拜访木

study. You don't have to go to India at all." Xuanzang asked him if they have *Yogacara-bhumi-sastra* because it was the scripture he especially wanted to study. In ancient India it was believed widely that the classic was an important sutra dictated by Maitreya. Out of his expectation, the old monk replied thoughtlessly, "Why ask for the book with wrong outlook? A real Buddhist will not study such a book." The reply insulted Xuanzang and he immediately retorted, "*Yogacara-bhumi-sastra* was dictated by Maitreya in person. You belittled it with wrong outlook. Don't you dread falling to the bottom level of the hell?"

Since Mokslagupta scorned his Buddhist accomplishments, Xuanzang asked the old monk, "Do you understand all the books you mentioned?" The old monk was still arrogant, "I am proficient in these books." Then Xuanzang asked questions by quoting content of *Abhidharmakosa-sastra*. Out of everyone's expectation, Mokslagupta offered wrong answers. Xuanzang raised another question and the old monk could not explain clearly and argued there was no such sentence in the book. The king's uncle, who was a dignitary was there too, proved the sentence was in the book. Then they took out the scripture for validation and confirmed Mokslagupta was wrong. The monk was ashamed of that and excused himself, "I am too old to remember all of these." Since then he respected Xuanzang

叉毱多，这位老僧只以普通的礼节对待他，并不认同他的佛学修养。木叉毱多傲慢地对玄奘说："我们这里一切佛经都有，足够你学习，不必很辛苦地跑到印度去。"玄奘问这里有没有《瑜伽师地论》，因为这是他特别想了解的大乘佛学经典，在古代印度，人们普遍相信这是一部由弥勒菩萨口述的重要经书。哪知老僧随口回答说："为什么问这种观点不正确的书呢？真正的佛门弟子是不会学习它的。"这个回答侮辱了玄奘严肃的信仰，他认为这位老僧的佛学修养不好，马上质问："《瑜伽师地论》是弥勒菩萨亲口所讲，你贬低它是观

新疆库车的苏巴什故城，是古代龟兹寺庙遗址，玄奘曾在这里讲说佛法。
Subashi Ancient City, Kuqa, Xinjiang. The site of ancient Qiuci temples where Xuanzang gave lectures on Buddhism.

very much.

Xuanzang and his companions were blocked by heavy snow and stayed in Qiuci for more than two months. He sometimes came to Mokslagupta and the old monk purposely dodged him and told the others privately, "The Chinese monk is hard to handle. If he goes to India, I am afraid the young Buddhists there cannot compete with him."

When the road was clear, Xuanzang left Qiuci. Two days later, they met more than 2,000 Turki cavalries trying to rob their properties. However, the robbers fought with each other in disagreement on the property division and fled to different directions. Xuanzang and his companions escaped much harm.

Xuanzang kept on his journey westwards and came to the foot of the famous ice-covered mountain Lingshan Mountain (Peak Musuer of Tianshan Mountain) after crossing a small kingdom. It was the main road of the north foot of Congling, more than 7,000 meters above the sea level. Covered by snow all year, the mountain often had snow landslides and was hard to climb. There was no dry area for camping. They had to hang the pan when cooking and slept on the ice. It took seven days for Xuanzang to get out of the mountain with about 30 percent casualty in his party and higher casualty proportion of horses. Then they reached the territory of

点不正确的书，难道就不怕掉到地狱的最底层去吗？"

因为这位老僧蔑视他的佛学修养，玄奘就问老僧："您说的那些经书，您都了解吗？"老僧仍然傲慢地说："我都完全明白。"于是玄奘便引用《俱舍论》的内容提问，不知道什么原因，木叉毱多居然答错了；玄奘再提出一条，老僧也无法讲明白，便说经书里面没有这句话。国王的叔叔是一位高僧，正好也在现场，站出来证明经书里确实有这句话。于是大家取出经书当场对证，证明木叉毱多的说法是错误的。这位老僧很惭愧，找借口说："我年纪大，忘掉了。"从此之后，他对玄奘就非常尊重。

因为大雪封锁了道路，玄奘等人在龟兹国停留了两个多月。他有时去找木叉毱多谈论，这位老僧居然躲着不敢见他，还私下里对人说："这个中国僧人很不好对付，

龟兹故城
Ancient city of Qiuci.

the West Turk.

At that time the West Turk enjoyed great influence and controlled more than 40 states in the West Region. After a long distance, Xuanzang reached the capital of West Turk Suy-ab (near Tokmak of Kirghizia). Later it became an important border town of Tang. What's more, it was probably the hometown of Li Bai (701–762), the great poet of China. However, this happened long after Xuanzang's

冰雪覆盖的天山
Snow-covered Tianshan Mountain.

他要是到印度去,印度年轻一辈的佛学人物恐怕都不是他的对手。"

等到大雪过后道路畅通时,玄奘就离开了龟兹。走了两天,忽然遇到突厥强盗,有2000多骑兵,要抢走玄奘他们的所有财物。可是这些强盗在商量怎样分配财物时,意见不统一,竟然自己打了起来,四散而去。玄奘等人幸运地躲过了一场灾难。

玄奘继续西行,路过一个小国,然后来到了著名的冰山——凌山(现在天山的穆素尔岭)脚下。这里是葱岭的北麓的交通要道,海拔7000多米,常年积雪,还不时发生雪崩,险峻而难行。在这里根本找不到干燥的地方可以停留,做饭时得把锅吊起来,睡觉时也只能躺在冰上。玄奘一行走了七天才走出这片冰山,损失惨重,十分之三四的人死在了路上,马匹等牲口的损失比例更高。过了这座冰山,他们就进入了西突厥境内。

当时西突厥的势力很大,西域40多个国家都受其控制。玄奘经过长途跋涉,来到了西突厥的国都碎叶城(在现在吉尔吉斯斯坦的托克马克市附近)。这里后来成为唐朝重要的边防城市,同时,它很可能是中

Li Bai

Li Bai was a great romantic poet born in Tang Dynasty, and one of the most outstanding poets in the history of China, nicknamed Poet Transcendent. He was born in Suy-ab and moved to Sichuan later. He was famous for his extravagant imagination and unconstrained poems. He was good at absorbing materials from the folk songs and myths and developed a unique magnificent style. He once lived in Chang'an and was recognized by Emperor Xuanzong (685–762) of Tang Dynasty. He was forced to leave Chang'an later. He spent most of his life travelling.

visit. It was a small and desolated town. He met Khan and his cavalry there who were hunting.

Khan was very polite to Xuanzang and invited him to the marquee after hunting. The marquee was decorated luxuriously. Khan and his ministers sat on the thick carpet, drinking wine made of horse milk. They prepared an iron chair especially for Xuanzang covered with thick cushion and offered him wine. Xuanzang stayed there for several days and started his journey again. Khan issued him the passport and appointed a young man who was in proficient in Chinese and languages of West Region states as the interpreter of Xuanzang to escort Xuanzang to Kāpiśa (Begram, northwest of Kabul, Afghanistan).

李白

　　李白是中国唐代伟大的浪漫主义诗人，也是中国历史上最卓越的诗人之一，被后人称为"诗仙"。他出生于碎叶城，后来迁居到四川。他才华横溢，诗歌风格豪放洒脱，想象丰富，善于从民歌、神话传说中汲取素材，形成一种特有的瑰丽绚烂的风格。他曾经在唐都长安居住，得到唐玄宗（685—762）的赏识，但后来又被迫离开长安。他的一生大部分时间是在漫游中度过的。

国伟大的诗人李白（701—762）的故乡。但这都是玄奘来过这里以后很久的事情了。在玄奘到达的时候，这里还比较荒凉，是一座规模不大的土城。他在这里遇见了正在打猎的突厥可汗和他的骑兵部队。

　　可汗对玄奘相当客气，打猎回来，将玄奘请到他居住的大帐篷里。这个大帐篷的装饰奢侈华丽，可汗和他的大臣们都坐在厚厚的地毯上，饮马奶做成的酒。他们专门为玄奘准备了一把铁制的椅子，上面铺着厚厚的坐垫，给他喝的是葡萄美酒。玄奘停留了几天，准备继续前进。可汗给他颁发了护照，并找了一位通

Khan also tried to persuade Xuanzang not to go India with an interesting reason. He said, "It is very hot in India and even in October it is as hot as May here. You will probably be melted by the burning sun." Of course Xuanzang would not flinch because of such a reason.

Xuanzang headed west continuously after leaving Suy-ab and then turned to southeast to Pamirs again after crossing many small states and regions, including today's Kirghizia and Uzbekistan.

Pamirs is the famous ridge of world and Xuanzang was

表现唐朝大诗人李白出游场景的绘画，明崔子忠绘。
Painting describing Li Bai's journey, painted by Cui Zizhong, Ming Dynasty.

probably the first traveler to the plateau. He once walked along the northeast side when he came to the West Turk and now he was to cross the west side to India. The road ahead was still dangerous with high mountains and deep snow and he could not see even a single man for several days. Xuanzang reached the strategic pass Tiemen Pass (ancient city of Derbent, Uzbekistan) where was defended

晓汉语和西域各国语言的少年，任命他为翻译官，护送玄奘到迦毕试国（在现在阿富汗喀布尔西北的贝格拉姆）。可汗也劝玄奘不要前往印度，不过他的理由比较有趣，他说："印度天气炎热，十月天气还和我们这儿五月一样。看您这样的外表，到那里恐怕要被太阳晒得融化了。"但玄奘当然不会因为这个原因就退缩。

玄奘从碎叶城一路西行，又经过了许多小的国家和地区，就是现在的吉尔吉斯斯坦、乌兹别克斯坦一带，然后转向东南，重新登上了帕米尔高原。

帕米尔高原是有名的世界屋脊，玄奘很可能是世界旅行家中来到这里的第一人。他翻越冰山到西突厥去的时候，曾走过它的东北边，现在则准备经过它的西边到印度去。这一段路仍然山深路险，积雪很深，一连几天都看不见人烟。玄奘来到险要的隘口铁门关（现在乌兹别克斯坦的德尔本特古城和要塞），这里有突厥士兵把守。玄奘出示突厥可汗颁发的护照之后，顺利通过了关口。

从铁门关往南到北印度边境为止，现在属于阿富汗，古代叫吐火罗国。在玄奘经过时，那里分布着许多国家和部落，其中有一个叫活国(在现在阿富汗北

by Turki soldiers. Xuanzang crossed the pass smoothly after presenting the passport issued by Turki Khan.

The area south to Tiemen Pass to the border of north India belongs to Afghanistan today, which was named Tukha'ra in the ancient time. There were many states and tribes when Xuanzang passed through the area. One of those was a state named Huoguo (near Kunduz, north of Afghanistan). The king was the eldest son of Turki Khan Dadu, whose wife was the younger sister of the king of Gaochang. Xuanzang had the autographed letter from the king of Gaochang. Unfortunately Gaochang princess had died at that time and Dadu was sick. When he learned Xuanzang came from Gaochang and when he read the letter, he could not help but thinking about his dead wife and crying with his children. He asked Xuanzang to stay and he would send Xuanzang to India in person when he recovered. Xuanzang then stayed in Huoguo State.

Who would have thought an astounding tragedy happened in the palace of Huoguo State. Dadu's new queen had an affair with his eldest son, the child of Dadu, and they poisoned Dadu. After Dadu's death, his eldest son acceded to the throne. In accordance with Turki customs, the new king married his step-mother. Xuanzang stayed there for more than one month because of the tragedy.

Xuanzang came to the new king for exchanging horses

帕米尔高原风光
Scene of Pamirs.

and an envoy as a guide to continue his journey to India. The new king directed him to a small kingdom Fuheluo Kingdom (west to Mazar-e Sharif, Afghanistan) controlled by Huoguo State, which was near to Amu Darya River on the north and had developed Buddhism. At that time dozens of monks from Fuheluo Kingdom were going back and they told Xuanzang there was a better road to India. Then Xuanzang came to Fuheluo Kingdom.

There were many Buddhist temples in the capital of Fuheluo Kingdom. The towers were normally decorated with gold on the top and looked luxuriant and solemn in the sun. The city was named Lesser Rajagriha. Pajagriha (Patna, Bihar of India) was the holy land of Buddhism and the place where Sakyamuni cultivated himself according to the doctrines. Xuanzang met a monk from the North India in Fuheluo Kingdom, called Huixing by Chinese. Huixing was learned and they admired each other after talking. Xuanzang lived there for more than one month and discussed with Huixing on Buddhist scriptures. We can say from that time Xuanzang had started the China-India cultural exchanges.

After leaving Fuheluo Kingdom, Xuanzang crossed two small countries together with Huixing. At that time they headed southeast and entered to a large snow-covered mountain (a mountain of Hindu Kush, Afghanistan). The road was very hard and dangerous, even more

部的昆都斯附近），国王是突厥可汗的大儿子呾度。呾度的妻子是高昌国王的妹妹，玄奘带来了高昌国王的亲笔信。可是很不巧，这时高昌公主已辞世，呾度自己也正在生病。他听说玄奘从高昌来，又看到书信，想起亡妻，与儿女等人不禁哭了起来。他请玄奘留下来，等他病好之后，要亲自送玄奘到印度去。玄奘就在活国停留下来。

哪知就在这个时候，活国发生了一件令人惊骇的宫廷惨剧。呾度新娶的王妃比较年轻。他在高昌公主之前还娶过一个妻子，他与这个妻子所生的大儿子与年轻的王妃私通，用毒药害死了呾度。呾度死后，高昌公主所生的儿子年龄还小，于是大儿子就当了国王，并按照突厥风俗，娶了他的后母。因为活国发生了这些事情，玄奘就在那儿停留了一个多月。

玄奘去见新国王，请求给他换一些马匹，并委派使臣带路，以便继续前往印度。新国王指引他去活国所控制的一个小国缚喝罗国（在现在阿富汗的马扎里沙里夫以西），说那儿北临阿姆河，佛教也很发达。正好有几十个缚喝罗国来的僧人要回去，他们告诉玄奘，从该国到印度另有好走的大路，不必再绕回活

dangerous than Lingshan Mountain and the desert he covered. Fortunately Xuanzang had rich experiences and equipment to cope with execrable natural conditions.

They crossed more than 600 *li* (300 km) in the snow-covered mountain and reached Ba'miyan (nearby Bamiyan of Afghanistan). Ba'miyan was a mountainous country with its capital located in the valley. The king received Xuanzang in person and invited him to live in the palace for days. After talking with Xuanzang, two dignitaries in the country marveled that there was such a dignitary in the east. They showed Xuanzang around warmly. In the valley northeast to the capital, Xuanzang saw two huge Buddha statues, majestic and vivid. The Buddha statue on the west was 150 *chi* high and the one on the east was more than 100 *chi*. Between the Buddha statues there was a temple where a bronze recumbent Buddha was as long as 1,000 *chi*. It was said these Buddha statues were created by outstanding experts. Xuanzang highly praised these Buddha statues.

Now we know these stone

长途跋涉的行脚僧，该图发现于敦煌藏经洞。
Wandering monk. The painting was discovered in Cangjing Grotto (Grotto for scripture storage), Dunhuang.

国。于是，玄奘便到了缚喝罗国。

缚喝罗国的都城中有很多佛教寺庙，塔顶上一般都用黄金装饰，太阳一照，光耀夺目，显得非常华丽庄严。这里号称"小王舍城"——王舍城（现在印度比哈尔邦的巴特那）是佛教圣地，即佛祖释迦牟尼修行的地方。玄奘在缚喝罗国遇到一位北印度来的僧人，中国人称他为慧性。慧性博学多才，与玄奘相谈之后，彼此都很尊敬和佩服对方。玄奘在这里住了一个多月，与慧性进行佛学方面的探讨。可以说，从这里开始，他已经在进行中印两国文化的交流工作了。

玄奘离开缚喝罗国后，与慧性作伴，又去了两个小国。这时他们的方向变成向东南而行，进入一座大雪山（现在阿富汗兴都库什山脉的伊拉克斯奇山），这一段路非常艰险，甚至比他之前走过的凌山、大沙漠还要凶险。好在玄奘已有了不少应付恶劣自然条件的经验和装备。

他们在大雪山中走了600多里，来到梵衍那国（在现在阿富汗的巴米扬附近）。梵衍那国是一个山国，都城也在山谷之中。玄奘到了都城，国王亲自出来迎接，请他到王宫住了几天。该国有两位高僧，与玄奘

statues of Buddhas were the renowned Buddhas of Bamiyan. *Chi* was the length unit of China, and three *chi* in Tang equals to 1 meter. We know the Buddhas of Bamiyan were 53 meters and 37 meters high respectively, indicating Xuanzang's record was precise. Unfortunately these two 1,500-old statues of Buddha were destroyed in March 2001. It was what Xuanzang who sought the gospel of Buddhism reverently could never image.

Departing Ba'miyan they kept their journey southeastwards. They were stuck by the heavy snow when they had nearly crossed the snow-covered mountain and got lost. They hid in the cove to avoid the wind and snow and kept on after the storm broke. After crossing the mountain they were facing Heiling (a mountain on the south part of Hindu Kush, Afghanistan). On the other side of Heiling was the territory of Kapisa. Heiling was the dividing line between the Middle Asia and India. Turki Khan's escort told Xuanzang their mission was concluded when Xuanzang reached the dividing line and the young interpreter departed Xuanzang and returned.

Kapisa was a large country northwest to India and the capital was near Kabul. The king professed Buddhism and received Xuanzang in person at the city gate with a number of monks. There were more than 100 temples in the capital and all tried to invite Xuanzang to live in their temple. One temple was named Zhizi Temple (Hostage

阿富汗兴都库什山下的村落
Villages at the foot of Hindu Kush, Afghanistan.

相谈之后，惊叹东方竟然有这样一位高僧。他们热情地带玄奘到处参观。在都城东北的山谷中，玄奘看到山壁岩石上雕刻着两尊高大的佛像，气魄雄伟，神态生动。西边的一座高150尺，东边一座高100多尺。两座佛像中间有一所寺院，寺内有一座铜制的卧佛像，更是长达1000尺。据介绍，这些佛像都出自名家之手。玄奘对这些大佛像十分赞叹。

Wrecked Bamiyan Buddha, Afghanistan.

Temple) which was said to be built for a prince hostage of the Han Dynasty. The monk of the temple said, "Our temple was built for the prince of Han. Now you, master, come from China and should first live in our temple." Xuanzang accepted the invitation.

After investigating, Xuanzang believed the prince was probably the son of Dou Rong, early Eastern Han (25–220). Dou Rong once ruled Hexi area (area of Gansu and Qianghai west to the Yellow River). In order to establish a tie with the neighbor state, he probably sent his son as a hostage. It was said there were no pears or peaches in

现在我们知道，这两座石刻的大佛像，就是著名的巴米扬大佛。尺是中国的长度单位，唐代的3尺约相当于1米。按照现代人的测量结果，两座巴米扬大佛的高度分别是53米和37米，可见玄奘的记载相当准确。但令人遗憾的是，在2001年3月，这两座具有约1500年历史的大佛像被摧毁了。这是虔诚追求佛法真理的玄奘法师不可能想到的。

离开梵衍那国，玄奘等人继续向东南走。将要走完大雪山时，又遇到大雪，迷失了道路。他们在山坳中躲避风雪，天亮后再赶路前进。出了大雪山，前面是一道黑岭（现在阿富汗兴都库什山脉南段的一座大岭）。过了这座山，就进入了迦毕试国境。黑岭是中亚与印度的分界岭，突厥可汗派人护送玄奘，声明就送到这里。在这里，那位少年翻译官辞别玄奘回去了。

迦毕试国是印度西北的一个大国，国都在现在的喀布尔附近。国王信奉佛教，亲自带众僧人出城门来迎接玄奘。都城之内有100多座佛寺，争着请玄奘去住。其中一座寺院名叫质子庙，据说是中国汉朝的一位王子在这里做人质时所造。这座庙的僧人说："我们的寺庙本是汉朝王子所造，现在法师从中国来，应

India. The prince planted these two kinds of fruit trees in person with the seeds he brought and therefore the local people had the pleasure to have the fruits.

Xuanzang and Huixing gave lectures on Buddhist scriptures in Mahayana temple and the king and the monks came to their lectures. The country had Buddhist leaders of Mahayana and Hinayana and they were not convinced by the other. Xuanzang was proficient both in Mahayana and Hinayana and could answer questions easily. All of them admired him very much.

Xuanzang was invited by the king of Tukha'ra and departed Huixing. After leaving Kapisa, Xuanzang walked more than 600 *li* (300 km) eastwards and climbed over Heiling. Finally Xuanzang reached India—the holy land in his mind. He was closer to his dream of getting Buddhist sutras from India.

该先住我们寺。"玄奘就答应了。

经过详细了解，玄奘认为，这位王子很可能是东汉（25—220）初年窦融的儿子。窦融曾在河西（现在甘肃、青海两省黄河以西的地区）地区实行统治，为了结交邻国，很可能派他的儿子来做人质。据说印度以前没有梨子和桃子这两种水果，王子用带来的种子亲手种植，所以当地人也开始吃到梨子和桃子了。

玄奘和慧性法师又在大乘寺里一起讲佛法，国王及众僧都来听讲。该国有讲大乘的和讲小乘的佛学领袖，互相不服，而玄奘兼通大小乘，对众人所提的问题应答如流，于是大家都对他很佩服。

慧性法师被吐火罗的国王请了回去，与玄奘作别。玄奘离开迦毕试国，向东走了600多里，翻过黑岭，终于抵达了他心中的圣地印度，离西天取经的理想已经很接近了。

V

Study in India

Xuanzang arrived in North India after climbing over Heiling. At that time India was not unified and geographically divided into central, east, south, west and north parts, collectively named Five India. India was in the last peak time of Buddhism.

Xuanzang was not the first monk or traveler to India from China, but the first traveler covering Five India. He first entered into the North India, then the Central India and East India, from where he came to the South India along the east coastline and then the West India again and finally returned the Central India. In the trip he covered more than 70 countries, large or small. He visited the Buddhist temples and grottos along the trip and studied the Buddhist thought and arts and the customs of countries he crossed. He obtained rich experiences and information along the trip, and sometimes dangerous and life-threatening experiences. But all in all, the Buddhist cradle land gave him many pleasant surprises and gains.

5 留学印度

玄奘越过黑岭，进入北印度。当时印度还没有统一，从地理上来说，分成中、东、南、西、北五部，称为五印度。那时的印度正处于佛教最后一个兴盛时期。

玄奘并不是中国第一个到达印度的僧人或旅行家，但他是第一个周游五印度的旅行家。他所走的路线，是先进入北印度，然后转入中印度，再转入东印度，沿印度东海岸到南印度，又由南印度绕行西印度，最后回到中印度，途中经过了大大小小70多个国家。他到处探访佛寺和石窟，研习佛教的思想和艺术，了解印度各地的风土人情。他沿途的见闻和经历非常丰富，甚至有非常惊险、几乎丧失性命的经历。不过总的来说，印度这块佛教的发源地还是带给他许多惊喜和收获。

玄奘进入北印度，首先经过现在阿富汗东部的一

Xuanzang entered into the North India and covered some areas of today's east Afghanistan. Soon he reached the famous Buddhist city Fodinggu City (south to Jalalabad, Afghanistan) where the temple enshrined the parietal bone of Sakyamuni.

Nearby there was a Lamplight City (southwest to Jalalabad, Afghanistan). Outside of the city there was a grotto where it was said that Sakyamuni defeated a dragon and left the shadow of Buddha on the stone wall. After hearing about that, Xuanzang found an old man as his guide to the grotto. The road was isolated and they met five robbers who carried blades. When they learned that Xuanzang was to worship the Buddha shadow, they followed Xuanzang out of curiosity. It was too dark to see anything in the grotto. Xuanzang paid homage to the east stone wall several hundreds of times, according to the old man's direction. Suddenly a silhouette appeared on the stone wall, dressed in cassock. Besides the silhouette, there were faint shadows of the others. That shocked all of them and the five robbers immediately decided to throw down their weapons and convert to Buddhism.

According to modern scholars, the Buddhist shadow was in fact a light reflection phenomenon under the special condition of grotto. The shadow Xuanzang and the others saw was actually their own. Of course Xuanzang did not understand this theory and he believed the

些地区。不久，便到了有名的佛教城市佛顶骨城（在现在阿富汗的贾拉拉巴德以南）。这里的寺院里供奉着佛祖如来的顶骨。

附近还有一个灯光城（在现在阿富汗的贾拉拉巴德西南），城外有一个石窟，据说当年佛祖在这里降伏了一条龙，并在石壁上留下佛影。玄奘听说后，就找了一个老人带路，前往参拜。这条路荒凉冷落，而且路上还遇到五个拿着刀的强盗，他们听说玄奘要去参拜佛影，也好奇地跟着一起走。石窟里什么也看不见，玄奘按老人的指点对着东面的石壁行礼参拜，拜了几百次，石壁上突然出现了一个身影，穿着袈裟，左右及背后还有其他模模糊糊的影子。这情形震撼了同来的人，五个强盗立即决定扔掉武器，接受佛法教导。

犍陀罗佛教艺术中的佛陀雕像
Buddha statues in Gandhara Buddhist Art.

shadows appeared because his piety moved Buddha.

Xuanzang headed southeast for more than 500 *li* (250 km) and reached Gandhara (Kabul River drainage area, Pakistan), where there was flower scent everywhere. The country once had developed Buddhism and famous Buddhist arts combining the Greek style and Indian style. When Xuanzang arrived, it had declined, with many precious Buddha statues left. The capital of Gandhara was Purushapura (Peshawar City, Pakistan). Many Buddhist masters who Xuanzang canonized, such as the important Mahayana theorists brothers Asanga and Vasubandhu (about 4th or 5th century), were born there.

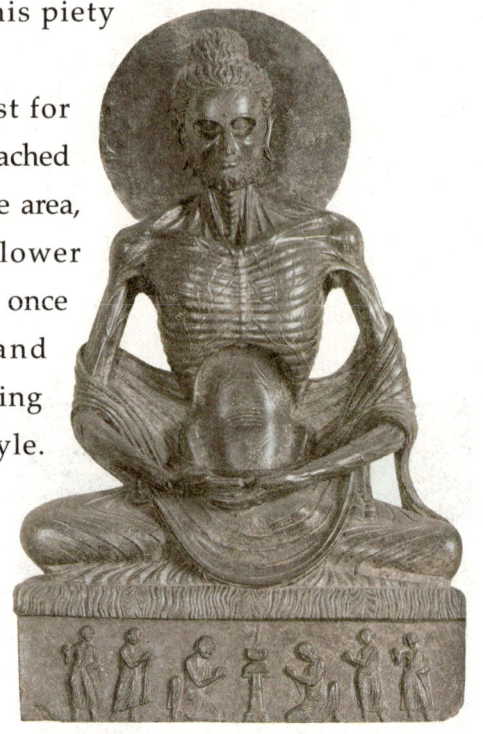

犍陀罗佛教艺术，苦行的释迦牟尼
Gandhara Buddhist Art, ascetic Sakyamuni.

Later Xuanzang visited some areas of Pakistan. However, the Buddhism was not that popular in those areas as before and the Buddhist temples and monks decreased a lot. At that time he heard that Kasmira (Kashmir) in North India was one of the Buddhist centers and decided to go there first.

根据现代学者的研究，所谓佛影，其实是在石窟这个特定的环境下产生的一种光学上的返光现象；玄奘等人所看到的佛影，就是他们自己的影子。当然，玄奘等人并不明白这种道理，他认为这是他的虔诚打动了佛祖。

玄奘向东南走了500多里，到达犍陀罗国（在现在巴基斯坦的喀布尔河流域），犍陀罗的意思是遍地花香。这个国家的佛教曾经很发达，产生了一种将希腊风格和印度风格相结合的著名佛教艺术。玄奘来到时，这里已经比较衰落，但还是留下许多珍贵的佛像等艺术遗迹。犍陀罗的都城叫布路沙布逻（现在巴基斯坦的白沙瓦城），玄奘所尊崇的许多佛教大师，比如大乘佛学的重要理论家无著、世亲（约4或5世纪）兄弟，就出生于这里。

此后，玄奘又经过了现在巴基斯坦的一些地区，所到之处，佛教信仰都已经不那么兴盛，佛教寺院和僧人都减少了很多。这时，他听说北印度有个迦湿弥罗国（现在的克什米尔），是佛学中心之一，就决定先到那儿去学习。

迦湿弥罗四面都是高山，玄奘沿着崎岖的栈道

Gandhara arts

It was a Buddhist art generated in Gandhara, northwest of ancient India around the 4th century BC after Macedonian King Alexander conquered India. The art was popular in the joint area of the India River and Kabul River and mainly reflected in the palace and temple buildings, Buddha sculpture and painting centering on Buddhism. On the basis of the traditional art of India, it absorbed the artistic expression of Greece, Persia and Rome and formed a new art style. Gandhara art had influenced India, Middle Asia, China and Japan.

Kasmira was bounded by high mountains and Xuanzang covered nearly 1,000 *li* (500 km) along the cragged plank road before he arrived in the country. The king professed Buddhism and sent his brother to receive Xuanzang at the border. After several days they reached the capital (Srinagar, Kashmir). The king met Xuanzang on an elephant and scattered flowers for him in person. The king invited Xuanzang to take the elephant with him. The towns there were splendid and Buddhist temples could be seen everywhere.

When learning Xuanzang came from afar for the Buddhist scriptures, the king arranged 20 copiers to copy the scriptures and invited a dignitary of nearly 70 years

犍陀罗艺术

产生于古代印度西北部犍陀罗一带的佛教艺术，其产生时间是在公元前4世纪马其顿国王亚历山大东征印度之后。犍陀罗艺术盛行于印度河与喀布尔河会合的区域，主要表现为宫殿寺庙建筑、佛像雕刻、绘画等，内容大多以佛教题材为主，在印度传统艺术的基础上，吸收希腊、波斯、罗马等地的艺术表现手法，从而形成一种新的艺术风格。犍陀罗艺术对印度、中亚、中国、日本等国都有影响。

走了将近1000里，才来到该国。迦湿弥罗国王崇奉佛教，派他的弟弟到边境来迎接玄奘。走了几天，来到该国都城（现在克什米尔的斯利那加），国王乘着大象来和玄奘相见，又亲自用手为他散花。国王请玄奘也乘大象进城。这里城郭壮丽，到处都有佛寺。

国王得知玄奘是远道前来取经，就派了20个抄写员专门为他抄写经书，又请一位年近七旬的高僧为他讲解。这位老僧名叫僧称，他不顾年老体衰，每天从早到晚热情传授。而玄奘学习也格外用心，领会得又快又深入。僧称对玄奘非常器重，对众人说："这

old named Sengcheng to explain it for him. Sengcheng gave lectures warmly from the morning to the night in spite of his old age and weakness. Xuanzang studied hard and mastered the essence quickly and thoroughly. Sengcheng valued Xuanzang highly and told the others, "The Chinese monk is talented and none of you can compare with him. He is good enough to pass on the traditions of the Vasubandhu brothers. It is pity he was born in the outlands far away and could not come here earlier to inherit the cause of the predecessors." Some famous monks were not convinced when they heard this and questioned Xuanzang with difficult questions. Xuanzang answered them clearly. All of them were convinced and felt ashamed.

Xuanzang stayed in Kasmira for about two years and improved his Buddhist knowledge and Sanskrit significantly. He also got familiar with the local dialects and laid a solid foundation for visiting Five India and translating the Buddhist scriptures.

In about 629, Xuanzang left Kasmira and covered a long distance before he reached T'akka (Punjab, Pakistan). Xuanzang and his companions met a gang of more than 50 robbers when they were crossing a forest. The gangsters robbed them of their belongings and drove them to a dry pond to murder them. Xuanzang and a young monk ran away nimbly. Hearing their suffering, a peasant who

位中国僧人才智出众,你们中没有人能赶得上。以他的资质,足以传承世亲兄弟的遗风。只可惜他生在远方的国家,没能早一点来到这里继承前辈圣贤的事业。"该国一些有名的僧人听到这话,觉得不服气,就提出一些疑难问题质问玄奘,而玄奘都回答得清楚明白。众人这才自愧不如。

玄奘在迦弥湿罗国停留了两年左右,佛学和梵文都大有长进,对当时印度人所说的各种语言也都逐渐熟悉,为周游五印度和翻译佛经打下了良好的基础。

大概在公元629年,玄奘离开迦弥湿罗,走了很久,出了克什米尔,来到磔(zhé)迦国(现在巴基斯坦的旁遮普省)。玄奘及其同伴经过一片大森林时,遇到了一伙有50多人的强盗。强盗们把他们的东西抢光,又把他们赶到一个干涸的池塘边,准备杀人灭口。玄奘与一个少年僧人机敏地逃跑了。一个正在耕地的村民知道他们的遭遇后,马上吹响海螺发出警报,80多个村民拿着棍棒赶来,把强盗们吓跑了。同伴们得救了,但因为财物被抢走,都很难过,只有玄奘微笑着,似乎无忧无虑。他劝慰大家说:"人最珍贵的是生命,既然生命还在,还有什么可以担忧的呢?"

was plowing blew the trumpet shell and more than 80 villagers rushed there with clubs. The gangsters were scared away and their companions were saved. However, they were sad because their belongings were robbed. Only Xuanzang smiled and seemed without worry. He comforted the others, "The most valuable thing is life. Since we are still alive, what can we worry about?"

The next day they reached a large city on the east of T'akka. A sainted Brahman man received him warmly and informed those in the city who were in belief of Buddhism to prepare food for Xuanzang. When the local robber leader heard that somebody robbed such a dignitary, he ordered each of his understrappers to present a bolt of cotton cloth to Xuanzang to express his regret. They presented more than 300 bolts of cloth and food and drinks to Xuanzang. Xuanzang took the chance to persuade them to give up evil and return to good. The robbers agreed. The Brahman was surprised at Xuanzang's influence and said this had never happened before. Xuanzang distributed the cotton cloth to his companions and the Brahman man and followed the old man to study Buddhist scripture for a month.

In this way Xuanzang traveled and studied before he arrived in the Central India. That year was 631 and he was 30 years old. Almost five years had passed since he left China. After crossing some countries he arrived in Kanya-

玄奘西天取经

　　第二天，玄奘到了磔迦国东部一座大城，有位德高望重的婆罗门老人热情招待了他，并派人通知城里信仰佛法的人为他做饭。当地的强盗首领听说有人抢了这样一位高僧的财物，为了表示歉意，便命令手下各自拿出一匹棉布，将300多匹棉布和饮食献给玄奘。玄奘趁机劝他们改邪归正，他们答应了。婆罗门老人对玄奘的感召力也很惊讶，说这种事以前从未发生过。玄奘把棉布分给同伴，又送了一些给婆罗门老

敦煌莫高窟第217窟壁画，表现佛居住的极乐世界歌舞升平的场景。
Fresco of NO.217 Grotto, Dunhuang Mogao Grottos, describing the scene of Elysium where Buddhas live.

kubja of the Central India. The capital was Sankasya (Kanauj, state of Uttar Pradesh, India).

Kanya-kubja was the political and cultural center of the whole India. On the west of Sankasya was the Ganges—the largest river of India. The city had a large population and many splendid buildings and gardens. People enjoyed a relatively high educational level and lived in prosperity. At that time the country was under reign of SIladitya (589–647), who was in his prime of life, wise and promising. He governed the country in perfect order and conquered the neighborhoods with Sankasya as the center. Many states of Five India obeyed his orders. SIladitya first professed Siva and then Buddhism and built many Buddhist pagodas, temples and supported many monks. Every five years, he presided a Wuzhe Meeting (Boundless Meeting, a religious assembly all sects can take part in), encouraging different sects to make academic discussion and exchanges. At the same time, SIladitya also loved literature and arts and composed several plays, which had been passed on until today.

When Xuanzang arrived, SIladitya was heading his troops in battle and Xuanzang did not meet him. Xuanzang lived there for some time and recorded information of the country. His record became the most reliable materials for the others to study India under the reign of SIladitya.

人，并跟着这位老人学习了一个月。

这就样，玄奘一路走，一路学习，渐渐来到了中印度。这时是公元631年，他已经30岁，离开中国也有差不多五年了。他经过一些国家，然后来到中印度的大国羯（jié）若鞠阇（shé），该国的都城叫曲女城（现在印度北方邦的卡瑙季）。

羯若鞠阇是当时整个印度的政治中心和文化中心。曲女城西面就是印度第一大河恒河。城中人口众多，居民生活富裕，有很多华丽的建筑和园林，人们的文化水平也比较高。那时统治羯若鞠阇的是有名的戒日王。戒日王正当壮年，英明有为，把国内治理得井井有条，进而以曲女城为中心，征讨四方，五印度很多国家都听从他的命令。戒日王原来信奉印度教湿婆派，后来又信奉佛教，修建不少佛塔、佛寺，并供养佛教僧众。每隔五年，由他主持举行一次无遮大会（各宗教派别均可参加的宗教大集会），鼓励各教派进行学术辩论和交流。同时，戒日王也喜爱文艺，写过好几种剧作，流传至今。

玄奘到的时候，戒日王正带领军队在外作战，玄奘没有见到他。玄奘在这儿住了一段时间，记录下这里的情况。他的记录成为后人研究戒日王统治时期印

Slladitya

Slladitya was the king of Kanya-kubja, North India and sat on a throne in 606. Under his reign, the country enjoyed strong national power. He unified North India centering on Sankasya. He set up another central regime of India following the Gupta Dynasty (about 320–540). He was also an important protector of Indian classical culture and supported many poets and writers. He loved literature and arts. He encouraged religious and academic exchanges among different sects. Xuanzang was received with great courtesy by the king when he visited India.

Xuanzang left Sankasya and kept on his journey. One time he and his companions, totaling more than 80 persons, took a large ship heading east along the Ganges. Suddenly dozens of small boats steered by robbers rushed from the woods on the banks and stopped them. The robbers anchored the ship at the bank and robbed all the passengers. These robbers professed a goddess and would kill a good-looking man each autumn as sacrifice to the goddess. This time they chose Xuanzang and were to kill him. Calmly, Xuanzang asked the robbers to allow him to read Buddhist scripture because he wished to be born again after his death to accomplish his wish of getting the Buddhist scripture, learn *Yogacara-bhumi-sastra* and convert these robbers. At that time, a strong wind swept

> **戒日王**
>
> 古代北印度羯若鞠阇国国王，公元606年即位。在他的统治下，该国国力强盛。他以首都曲女城为中心，征讨四方，基本统一北印度，建立了笈多王朝（约320—540）之后又一个印度中央政权。他也是印度古典文化的重要保护者，热爱文艺，扶持了不少诗人和作家，他本人也擅长文学创作。他鼓励各教派进行宗教学术交流，玄奘赴印期间，受到他的礼遇。

度情况的最可靠的资料。

玄奘离开曲女城继续旅行。有一次，他和同伴80多人乘一只大船顺着恒河向东前进，忽然两岸树林里面冲出十多只强盗的小船，将他们拦住。强盗把大船开到岸边，抢劫所有旅客。这些强盗信奉一位女神，每年秋天都要挑选一个相貌端正的人做牺牲品，杀了他祭祀女神。这次他们选中了玄奘，准备将他杀死。玄奘神色镇定，请求允许他念诵佛经，希望自己死后再次降生人间时，能够实现取经的心愿，学好《瑜伽师地论》，用来教化这些强盗。这时候正好刮起一阵很大的风，把河边的沙子都卷了起来，连树木都被吹

and wrapped sand at the river bank and broke the trees. The calm Ganges was rolling in immense surge and blew away or overturned the boats. The robbers were frightened. When they learned that Xuanzang was a monk coming from China for the Buddhist scriptures, they believed it was the goddess's will not to kill Xuanzang. They released him and apologized to him. Upon being educated by Xuanzang, the robbers gave up weapons, returned the properties they robbed and converted to Buddhism. So Xuanzang was lucky to avoid the tragedy

敦煌壁画《西方净土变》，描绘想象出来的佛国景象。
Amitabha's Pure Land, Fresco of Dunhuang, describing the Buddhist kingdom in mind.

断。同时平静的恒河变得波浪汹涌，船只都被吹得漂走，有的甚至被吹得翻转。强盗们很害怕，得知玄奘是从中国来求取佛经的僧人，他们认为一定是女神不允许他们杀害玄奘，就赶紧将他释放，向他忏悔道歉。经过玄奘的教诲，强盗们扔掉武器，把财物归还给旅客，并接受了佛教的戒律。就这样，玄奘很幸运地逃过了杀身之祸。这件奇异的事情传扬开来，玄奘获得了很大的名声。

玄奘脱险之后，继续旅行，路上很顺利。不久之后，他来到了佛祖释迦牟尼诞生的地方迦毗（pí）罗卫国。这个地方在现在的哪儿，存在争议，有人说是在现在尼泊尔的南部，有人说是在现在印度北方邦的北部。玄奘发现，这里早已衰败，到处是废弃倒塌的房屋和寺院，没有什么人。这种情景使他失望，于是他很快离开这里，前往心目中的又一个佛教圣地那烂陀寺。

在离开长安五年、历经千辛万苦之后，玄奘终于抵达当时印度的佛教最高学府那烂陀寺。这座寺院在当时的摩揭陀国（现在印度比哈尔邦的巴特那和加雅一带）。这时，他的名声早已传到那烂陀寺。听说他

of being killed. The experience was spread widely and Xuanzang received great reputation.

After coming through this danger, Xuanzang kept on his journey. Soon he arrived in Kapilavastu where Sakyamun was born. There are different opinions on where the place is. Some believe it is in the south of Nepal and some say it is in the north of state of Uttar Pradesh, India. Xuanzang found the country had declined and discarded and collapsed houses and temples could be seen everywhere. But nearly nobody could be seen. He was disappointed and left there soon to another holy land Nalanda Vihara.

After five years leaving Chang'an and numerous difficulties and dangers, Xuanzang finally arrived in the highest institution of learning of India—Nalanda Vihara. The temple was located in Magadha (Patna and Gaya, Bihar, India). His reputation had reached Nalanda Vihara already. The temple sent four dignitaries to meet him when they learned he was close to the temple. He was received ceremoniously, with 200 monks and more than 1,000 common people carrying the Buddhist instruments and scented flowers meeting the distinguished guest from Empire Tang.

Xuanzang was gratified with the fact that Buddhism was blooming. In the fiction *the Journey to West*, Tangseng's destination was Larger Leiyin Temple (Thunder Temple)

到了附近，寺里即派出四位高僧前去迎接。他抵达那烂陀寺的情景十分隆重，有200名僧人、1000多名民众拿着佛教的法器和香花前来迎接这位从唐帝国远道而来的贵客。

令玄奘欣慰的是，这里还是一派繁盛景象。在小说《西游记》中，唐僧取经的目的地是西天的大雷音寺，那里是佛祖如来和众多菩萨修行的地方，气势宏伟而华丽。这种描写，可能参考了关于那烂陀寺的记载。经过

那烂陀寺遗址
Site of Nalanda Vihara.

where Sakyamuni and Buddha cultivated themselves according to Buddhist doctrine. The description may be referred to the record on Nalanda Vihara. The temple was grand and splendid, built by kings of India. It was like a square town. The major building was three-stories high and the walls were decorated with the life-sized statues that were engraved exquisitely. The roof, eaves and ground of the temple were covered with special materials, strong and durable. The temple was divided into living quarters and the teaching section. Many Buddhist pagodas were distributed in the teaching section. Exquisite patterns were engraved on the surface of the pagodas, telling different Buddhist stories.

Nalanda Vihara had an amazing collection of books, reaching 9 million volumes at the peak time. The Buddhists and others studying in the temple totaled more than 10,000. Though it was a Buddhist academic center, scholars at the temple gave lectures on the other subjects. Each day more than 100 lectures were held on Buddhist classics, astronomy, mathematics and medicine and so on. It was home to scholars of the highest level of India in Buddhism and other sciences. The king ordered more than 100 towns in the neighborhood to support Nalanda Vihara. Each town had 200 households. In this way the scholars in the temple did not have to worry about food, cloth or lodging.

历代印度君王的营建,那烂陀寺规模宏伟壮观。它宛如一座方型的城,主要建筑高三层,围墙上面排列着与人一样大小的塑像,雕刻得很精细。寺院的房顶、房檐和地面都用特制的材料覆盖,坚实耐用。寺院建筑分为居住区和教学区。教学区散布着许多佛塔,塔的外面雕有精美的图案,表现各种佛教故事。

  那烂陀寺拥有数量惊人的藏书,据说最多的时候达到900万卷。在这里学习的佛教徒和其他民众,总数达1万人以上。这里虽然是佛教学术中心,但是也研究和传授其他学问,每天都有100多个讲座,讲授的课程包括佛教经典、天文学、数学、医药等。这里云集了当时印度水平最高的佛教和其他方面的学者。国王命令周围100多个城镇供养那烂陀寺,每个城镇有200户人家,这样一来,寺里的学者们就不必为吃饭、穿衣、休息等方面的花费而操心了。

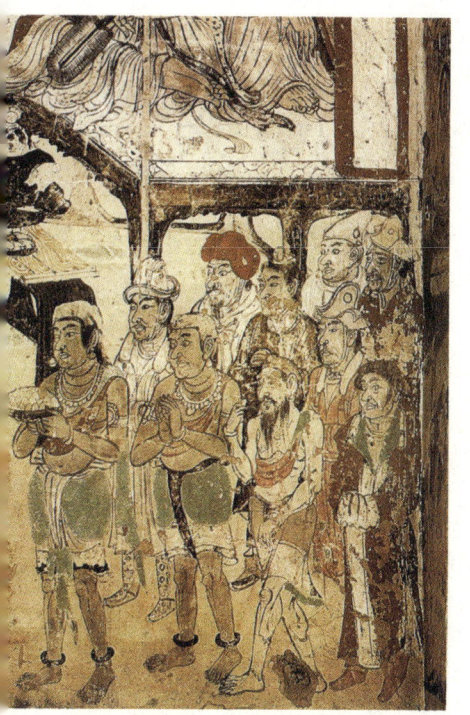

敦煌莫高窟壁画,手持供奉之物的各国供养人
Fresco of Dunhuang Mogao Grottos, providers from different countries.

Xuanzang was brought to the head of the temple, the highest academic authority Shilabhadra. It was said that Shilabhadra was more than 100 years old at that time. Among the 10,000 disciples studying in the temple, more than 1,000 were proficient in 20 volumes of Buddhist scriptures; more than 500 were proficient in 30 volumes; about 10 were proficient in 50 volumes and only Shilabhadra was proficient in all of the Buddhist scriptures.

Xuanzang saluted to Shilabhadra with the highest respect in accordance with the rules. Shilabhadra asked where Xuanzang came from and why did he came to the temple. Xuanzang answered, "I come from China and I want to study *Yogacara-bhumi-sastra* under your tutorship." Upon hearing the answer, Shilabhadra was so exciting that he could not help but cry. The master's nephew was a dignitary of more than 70 years old. He explained that three years ago Shilabhadra contracted a disease so miserable that he nearly committed suicide. Then he had a dream in which Bodhisattva told him to wait until a Chinese monk who would come to study *Yogacara-bhumi-sastra* and spread the studies to the remote areas. Shilabhadra waited for the Chinese monk against the pains. Xuanzang's visit proved his dream so Shilabhardra was so excited. All these others believed it must be Bodhisattva's arrangement for Xuanzang to

玄奘被带去见那烂陀寺的寺主、最高学术权威戒贤法师。这个时候，戒贤法师据说已100多岁了。当时在寺里学习的上万人中，通晓20部经书的有1000多人，通晓30部经书的有500多人，通晓50部经书的只有十个人左右，至于通晓所有经书的，就只有戒贤一个人。

玄奘按照规定，向戒贤法师行了最尊敬的礼。戒贤问他从哪里来，到这里做什么，他回答："我从中国来，想跟着您学习《瑜伽师地论》。"听到这话，衰老而多病的戒贤法师突然激动地哭起来。法师的侄子是一位70多岁的高僧，向大家解释说，三年前，戒贤法师突然得了一种痛苦的怪病，他几乎想绝食自杀。那时他梦到菩萨对他说，希望他能等一个中国来的僧人跟他学习《瑜伽师地论》，将这部经典传播到遥远的地方。戒贤法师就这样忍受着痛苦，等待中国僧人出现；而玄奘的到来，正好验证了他的梦，因此戒贤法师才这样激动。众人也都认为，让玄奘跟随戒贤学习，是菩萨的安排。

玄奘开始了在那烂陀寺的留学生活。那烂陀寺藏书丰富，给他提供了便利的学习条件。这里学术风气良好，戒律严格。他跟其他僧人一样，选修各种课

follow Shilabhadra.

Xuanzang started his study in Nalanda Vihara. The rich collection of books offered him an easy place to study. The academic climate there was excellent and the commandment was strict. Xuanzang took different courses as the other monks and wanted to waste no time at all.

Because he was an international student or highly evaluated by Shilabhadra, Xuanzang enjoyed the highest level of treatment in the temple. He was arranged a nice chamber and rich food, including a kind of special large rice which tasted very good, was produced only in Magadha and offered only to the king and senior monks. He did not need to take care of the sundries that the common monks had to do and had two servants. He could take the elephant with luxurious seat. Only about ten monks in the temple enjoyed such treatment.

After settling in Nalanda Vihara, Xuanzang visited the Buddhist scenic spots nearby. He visited Rajgir and Griddhkuta where Sakyamuni cultivated himself and preached the Buddhist scriptures. He saw a pagoda named Dayan Pagoda (Giant Wild Goose Pagoda) on a mountain. It was said the monks there professed Hinayana, which allowed the eating of meat. One day they could not find food anywhere and the monk who was in charge of food preparation joked about a flock of giant

印度比哈尔帮巴拉贡村的玄奘纪念堂内的彩绘棚顶
Color painting of the ceiling of Xuanzang Memorial Hall, Barragon Village in Bihar, India.

程,每一点时间都不愿意浪费。

或许是由于他特殊的留学身份和戒贤法师对他的器重,玄奘在寺里享受到了几乎是最高规格的待遇。他被安排住在级别很高的房间,每天得到丰富的食物,其中有一种特别的稻米,颗粒很大,味道特别好,只有摩揭陀这一带出产,国王和高级僧侣才可以

wild geese flying by. "Bodhisattva, you should know we had nothing to eat today," he said. Before he had finished his words, a goose fell down from the sky and died. The monks, shamed and scared, believed that Bodhisattva must have sacrificed himself to instruct them. Since then they decided to transfer to Mahayana and never eat meat. They buried the goose and built Dayan Pagoda. The story moved Xuanzang deeply.

After Xuanzang returned to Nalanda Vihara, Shilabhadra gave lectures on *Yogacara-bhumi-sastra* in person for Xuanzang. It was the most authoritative works of Mahayana. Xuanzang came afar to India was to study the scripture thoroughly. The sutra was obtuse and hard to understand. It was also very long, totaling more than 40,000 pieces, with each piece containing four sentences with complete meaning. Later Xuanzang translated it into Chinese to more than 100 volumes. At that time, the scripture study was conducted in the way that the teacher cited the scripture paragraph by paragraph

玄奘纪念堂前的玄奘雕像
Xuanzang statue in front of Xuanzang Memorial Hall.

享受供应。他不必去做僧人们应该承担的各种杂事，还配备有两个专门的仆人，出行时可以骑坐上面安设着华丽座位的大象。整个寺院享受这种待遇的人，只有十个左右。

在那烂陀寺安顿下来之后，玄奘又到附近的佛教胜地去游览。他参观了佛祖修行、传道的地方王舍城、灵鹫山等地。他游览一座山时，看到山上有座塔，叫大雁塔。据说从前这里的僧人修行小乘佛教，是吃肉的，有一天哪里也找不到食物，负责准备食物的僧人就对天上飞过的一群大雁开玩笑说："菩萨啊，你应该知道我们今天没有食物可吃。"刚说完，就有一只大雁从高空冲下来摔死了。僧人们又惭愧又害怕，认为这是菩萨牺牲自己来教导他们。他们决定从此修行大乘佛教，不再吃肉。他们把这只大雁埋葬好，并修了这座大雁塔。这个故事使玄奘深受感动。

回到那烂陀寺之后，戒贤法师开始亲自为玄奘讲授《瑜伽师地论》。《瑜伽师地论》是大乘佛教最权威的著作，玄奘来西天取经，主要就是想透彻地了解这部经书。这部经书极为深奥难懂，篇幅也很长，用梵文计算，有4万颂之多，颂是梵文的量词，每颂通常

and stopped to make explanation whenever a student had a question until the student understood it thoroughly. It took more than one year for Shilabhadra to explain the sutra for one time thoroughly. Even Xuanzang, who was talented and had strong perception, had to listen to him three times to understand and master the scriptures. In addition to *Yogacara-bhumi-sastra*, Xuanzang studied the other sutras and knowledge.

Xuanzang spent five years in Nalanda Vihara. When the overseas study was to conclude, he became one of the ten monks who were proficient in 50 volumes of scriptures.

About 500–600 years later, Nalanda Vihara was destroyed in the war. It was discovered in the middle of 19th century. In 1950s, the Chinese government donated money and the design drawings to build Xuanzang Memory Hall of Chinese near the site of Nalanda Vihara to mark the much-told story of the China-India cultural exchange history.

包括具有完整意思的四句话；后来玄奘将它翻译成中文，则多达100卷。当时学经的方式，是由老师把经书一段一段地背出来，如果学生有疑问，就停下来解答，直到完全理解为止。戒贤法师为玄奘讲解这部经书，讲一遍就需要一年多的时间。即使是玄奘这样天姿聪颖、领悟力很强的人，也认真学了三遍，才真正掌握这部经书。除了《瑜伽师地论》，他还学习了很多别的经书和其他知识。

玄奘在那烂陀寺度过了大约五年的留学生涯，到留学生涯快结束时，他已经成为能够通晓50部经书的十个人里面的一个。

大概五六百年后，那烂陀寺毁于兵火。从19世纪中叶开始，它才重新被人们发掘出来。20世纪50年代，中国政府捐赠一笔钱和设计图纸，在那烂陀寺遗址附近建了一座中国风格的玄奘纪念堂，以纪念这段中印文化交流史上的佳话。

VI

Eloquent Chinese Master

After his learning at the Nalanda Temple came to an end, Xuanzang left the temple, and continued his journey to India. On his way, he paid a visit to a famous temple, where enshrines a sandalwood statue of Avalokitesvara Sitting Leisurely, which is said to be very efficacious. Some people would often come here, without eating or drinking for seven or 14 days to make all kinds of prayers to the Buddha. Xuanzang also bought a lot of flowers and twisted them into a garland, piously visited the statue, and made three wishes: firstly, upon accomplishment of his learning, he can return to China safe and sound; secondly, he hopes he could be born beside the Maitreya Bodhisattva; thirdly, he hopes to have Buddha-nature, and be able to eventually become a Buddha through self-cultivation. These were what he concerned about most.

He came to East India from Central India. Having heard of a Simhalauipa (meaning the country of lion tamers,

6

雄辩的中国法师

《观音图》,南宋法常绘。观音又称观自在。
Painting of Kwan-yin, painted by Fachang, South Song Dynasty.

在那烂陀寺的学习告一段落之后,玄奘离开寺院,继续他的五印度之旅。在路上,他到一座有名的庙宇去参观,庙里供奉着一尊檀木雕刻的观自在菩萨像,据说非常灵验。经常有人到这里来,七天或十四天不吃不喝,向菩萨提出种种祈愿。玄奘也买了很多鲜花,做成花环,虔诚地参拜菩萨像,并许了三个心愿:第一,学成之后可以平安无事地回到中国;第二,希望来生能够出生在弥勒菩萨的身边;第三,希望自己有佛性,能够通过修行最终

now Sri Lanka) on the seas, he intended to head for the country. A monk from South India advised him that it was a very dangerous marine journey from here, and that he could go to the southeast corner of South India from where he could reach Simhalauipa by water in three days. Therefore, Xuanzang traveled along the east coast of India to Dravida (now Kanchipuram of Tamil Nadu in India) in the South India), where he met hundreds of monks from Sinhala. Originally, the country suffered from famine, so they fled to India. Xuanzang asked to learn from *Yogacara-bhumi-sastra* from them, but their insights were not beyond what Shilabhadra had described.

Xuanzang traveled northwestward to West India along with some Sinhalese monks. Later, they reached Parvata (now Harappa of Punjab province in Pakistan) in North India, where there were several very learned monks. Xuanzang thus stayed to learn from them for two years.

He returned to Central India, and returned to the Nalanda Temple to visit his teacher Master Shilabhadra, and then he traveled around to visit renowned masters and consulted them modestly. He went to visit another Buddhist master Jayasena, a Grha-pati with profound erudition in astronomy, geography, medicine, and mathematics, in addition to the theories of various Buddhist schools. He was not only learned, but also boasted high morality and was respected by people.

成佛。这是他最牵挂的几件事。

他由中印度来到东印度，听说海上有个僧伽罗国（意思是驯狮人之国，即现在的斯里兰卡），打算前往。有个南印度的僧人劝他说，从这里出发海路很险恶，不如到南印度的东南角，从那儿水路三天就可以到僧伽罗国。于是玄奘沿印度东海岸来到南印度的达罗毗荼国（现在印度泰米尔邦的康契普腊姆）。在这里他遇到了几百名来自僧伽罗的僧人，原来该国发生饥荒，所以他们逃到印度来。玄奘向他们请教《瑜伽师地论》，见解也并没有超过戒贤所说。

玄奘与一些僧伽罗僧人结伴，又绕行西北，到西印度。后来到达北印度的钵伐多国（现在巴基斯坦旁遮普省的哈拉巴），那儿有几个很有学问的高僧，玄奘就停留下来，跟着他们学习了两年。

他回到中印度，回那烂陀寺看望了一下老师戒贤法师。然后又到处去拜访名师，虚心请教。他去拜访另一位佛学大师胜军。胜军是一位居士，学问渊博，除佛教各派理论外，天文、地理、医学、数学等样样精通。胜军不但学问精深，而且品德也受世人推崇，摩揭陀国国王和戒日王先后邀请他担任国师，他都拒绝了，说：

King of Magadha and King Harshavardhana invited him in succession to act as a country guru, but he refused, saying, "To accept generous treatment from others, one should be concerned about some things for them. I am now busy with getting rid of life and death troubles, how can I have time to spend on your state affairs?" Xuanzang followed Jayasena a year or two, making his learning more profound.

One day, Xuanzang dreamed that the Nalanda temple became deserted and empty without anyone, and that the town outside the temple was burnt to ashes. He told his dream to Jayasena, feeling it was an ominous sign.

After eight-months of travel in other places, Xuanzang returned to the Nalanda Temple. Shilabhadra asked him expound to others the Mahayana doctrines of Vasubandhu and Asanga et al. At that time, Simha-rasmi, another eminent monk in the temple, gave lectures on *Madhyamika-sastra* and *Sata-sastra* written by Nagarjuna (about 2nd–3rd century). Nagarjuna's Mahayana doctrine theory was different from that of Vasubandhu and his brother, and Shi Ziguang took advantage of the theory of Nagarjuna to controvert the *Yogacara-bhumi-sastra*. Xuanzang was very familiar with Nagarjuna's writings and the *Yogacara-bhumi-sastra*, thinking that the two were not antagonistic, and can diffuse into each other, so he went to debate Simha-rasmi. Xuanzang had outstanding knowledge and

"接受人家的优厚待遇，就要替人家操心一些事情。我正忙着超脱生死烦恼，哪有时间管理国事呢？"玄奘跟着胜军又学习了一两年，学问更加精深。

有一天，玄奘做了一个梦，梦见那烂陀寺变得荒废，空无一人，而寺外的乡镇都被烧成了灰烬。他跟胜军说起这事，觉得是不祥之兆。

在其他地方又游历了八个月，玄奘重新回到那烂陀寺。戒贤让他为大家讲解世亲、无著等人的大乘理论。当时，寺中另一位高僧师子光已经给大家讲了龙树（约2—3世纪）所著的《中论》和《百论》。龙树的大乘理论与世亲兄弟有差异，师子光就借龙树的理论否定《瑜伽师地论》。玄奘对龙树的著作和《瑜伽师地论》都很熟悉，认为两者并不对立，可以融会贯通，就去跟师子光辩论。玄奘的学问和辩论才能出众，师子光说不过他，学生都转而来听玄奘的课。玄奘写了一部梵文著作《会宗论》3000颂，说明大乘理论两派之间并不互相违背，写成后给戒贤和大家看，得到一致称赞。师子光不服气，离开寺院，找了一个东印度来的高僧与玄奘辩论，但那位僧人一看玄奘的气势，竟然不敢开口。于是玄奘的声誉更高了。

debate talents, and Simha-rasmi was inferior to him in eloquence, so students turned to listen to the lectures of Xuanzang. Xuanzang wrote a Sanskrit book, showing that the two sects of the Mahayana doctrine theory did to run against each other. Upon completion, he showed his book to Shilabhadra and others, wining unanimous praise. Shi Ziguang was not convinced, so he left the temple, and found an eminent monk from East India to debate Xuanzang, but that monk did not dare to speak at the sight of the imposing manner of Xuanzang, thus sending Xuanzang's reputation higher.

Before Shi Ziguang left the temple, Nalanda Temple encountered trouble. King Harshavardhana passed through Udra (now Bhubaneswar of Orissa in India) in East India. The monks in Udra believed in Theravada Buddhism, and criticized Mahayana Buddhism for distorting the theories of Buddhas. They based their opinions on the *Debate on Mahayana Sastra* written by Prajnagupta who was a teacher of three generations of kings of a state in South India with a high status. King Harshavardhana wrote a letter to the Nalanda Temple, ordering the temple to send four persons to debate with the monks of Udra. Four persons, including Simha-rasmi and Xuanzang, were selected. The other three were worried, so Xuanzang comforted them and said that he was familiar with Theravada theory, thinking that it was

表现佛教辩论场景的《维摩诘图》，敦煌莫高窟103窟壁画。维摩称病在家，佛祖派遣文殊师利等弟子去探视，维摩宣扬大乘教义。
Portrait of Vimalakirti Giving Lectures on Buddhist Sutra. Fresco of No. 103 Grotto, Dunhuang Mogao Grottos. Vimalakirti was sick at home and Saykamuni sent Manjusri and the other disciples to visit him. And then Vimalakirti gave lectures on Mahayana.

在师子光还没离寺时，那烂陀寺遇到了一件麻烦事。原来，戒日王远征时经过东印度的乌荼国（现在印度奥里萨邦的布巴内斯瓦尔），该国的僧人信奉小乘佛教，抨击大乘佛教歪曲了佛的说法。他们所依据的是般若毱多所著的《破大乘论》700颂，这人是南印

insufficient to overturn Mahayana theory. He said he was willing to be alone in the debate, and said that even in the case of debate failure, it was be only the failure of him as a Chinese monk, and would not affect the reputation of the Nalanda Temple. Then King Harshavardhana wrote again to say that the debate would not be carried out for the time being.

Unexpectedly, a Loka'yata believer came to the temple, and asked to debate. Loka'yata believed in the four elements in nature—land, water, fire, and wind. The believer posted on the door 40 theories, claiming that if anyone could refute any of the 40 theories, he would cut off his head to apologize. Others were afraid of accepting the challenge. Xuanzang finally let a servant tear that paper and tread on it. He brought the Loka'yata believer before Master Shilabhadra et al, and after several debates, the believer was made to have nothing to say, and had to concede defeat. Xuanzang therefore punished him to serve as his servant.

Xuanzang made a research on the *Debate on Mahayana Sastra*, and found some doubts, so he consulted with the Loka'yata believer. The believer secretly explained the book to Xuanzang at midnight, and solved his doubts. Xuanzang found out the errors and *Debate on the Evil Opinions*, omissions of the book, and wrote another Sanskrit book with as many as 1,600 parts. After reading

度一个国家三代国王的老师，地位很高。戒日王写了封信给那烂陀寺，命令寺里派四个人去跟乌茶国僧人辩论。师子光、玄奘等四个人被选拔出来。其他三个人都很担心，玄奘安慰他们说，他熟悉小乘理论，认为该派理论不足以推翻大乘理论，他愿意独自前往辩论，即使辩论失败，也只是他这个中国僧人的失败，不会影响那烂陀寺的声誉。这时戒日王又写信来，这场辩论暂不进行。

不料又有一个顺世外道的信徒找上门来，要求寺里的人跟他论辩。顺世外道信奉自然界的地、水、火、风等四大元素，这位信徒在门上贴了40条理论，声称若有人驳倒其中一条，他就砍下自己的脑袋来谢罪。别人都不敢接受挑战，最后玄奘让仆人去将那张纸撕毁，还用脚踩。他把顺世外道信徒带到戒贤法师等人面前，经过反复几次辩论，顺世外道信徒被驳得无话可说，只好认输。玄奘就惩罚他做自己的奴仆。

玄奘研究《破大乘论》，有些地方有疑问，就向这位顺世外道信徒请教。这个人在半夜里偷偷向玄奘解说这部书，解决了他的疑点。玄奘找出《破大乘论》的错误和漏洞，写成了又一部梵文著作《破恶见论》，

the book, Master Shilabhadra and other eminent monks were pleased to praise, "Which rival cannot be defeated if we debate according to this book?"

Xuanzang let that believer regain his freedom. That person bid a farewell very happily, and went to Kamarupa (now Guwahati of Assam in India), saying to the King Kuma'ra (meaning child) that there was a Chinese Master in the Nalanda Temple with high morality, profound erudition, and sense of obligation. The King thus sent for Xuanzang.

At that time, a very good fortune-teller in the Nalanda Temple came to Xuanzang. Xuanzang asked about his remaining life and when he should return to China. That person gave vague answers. Xuanzang again asked how he could transport a great deal of Buddhist scriptures and statues he prepared to take to China? That person smiled and said King Harshavardhana and King Kuma'ra would help him. Xuanzang found it strange that he had not seen the two kings, so how could they help him? That person told him that King Kuma'ra had sent for him. If he could see King Kuma'ra, he could also see King Harshavardhana.

Xuanzang started to pack his luggage, and wrapped Buddhist scriptures and statues tightly. Nalanda Temple monks were reluctant to let him go, and came to advise him not to leave. They went to Master Śīlabhadra, and Śīlabhadra

有1600颂之多。戒贤大师和其他高僧看了,都高兴地称赞说:"依据这个去跟对方辩论,哪个对手能不惨败呢?"

玄奘让那个顺世外道信徒恢复了自由。那个人很高兴地告辞而去,跑到东印度的迦摩缕波国(现在印度阿萨姆邦的高哈蒂),对该国的鸠摩罗(意思是小孩子)王说,那烂陀寺有这样一个品德高尚、学问渊博、讲义气的中国法师。这位国王就派人来请玄奘。

当时那烂陀寺里有个擅长占卜算卦的人,突然来找玄奘。玄奘向他请教,自己寿命还有多长,何时应该回中国,这个人说得很含混。玄奘又问,自己准备带大量的佛经和佛像回国,应该怎么运送呢?这个人笑着说,戒日王和鸠摩罗王会派人帮他送回去。玄奘觉得奇怪,说自己跟这两位国王从没见过面,他们怎么会相助呢?那人就告诉他,鸠摩罗王已经派人来请他了,如果见到了鸠摩罗王,也就会见到戒日王。

玄奘开始整理行装,将佛经和佛像很严实地包装起来。那烂陀寺的僧人们都舍不得让他走,纷纷前来劝阻。大家到戒贤法师那儿去,戒贤问玄奘自己的意见,玄奘坚决地说:"我到佛国乐土来,是为了寻求佛

asked about the opinions of Xuanzang. Xuanzang said firmly, "I came to the Buddhist paradise in order to seek the true essence of Buddhism so as to benefit the people of my country. My trip has been rewarding, and I want to go back to translate these scriptures. This is my best repayment for my teachers and everyone." Master Shilabhadra said gladly, "This is also what I want you to do." So Shilabhadra told others not to advise Xuanzang to stay.

At that moment, the messenger sent by the King Kuma'ra arrived, and hoped that Shilabhadra could dispatch Xuanzang. Shilabhadra was worried that King Harshavardhana would send Xuanzang to participate in the debate, so he replied to King Kuma'ra, "China's monk has decided to return to his country, so he has no time to visit you." King Kuma'ra then sent his messenger to say, "Even if Xuanzang will return to his country, ask him to come to me before leaving. This is no problem, anyway. I hope the Chinese eminent monk can come without any further delay." Master Shilabhadra delayed to let Xuanzang see him, and King Kuma'ra flew into a rage. The king asked someone to deliver a letter with stern tones, saying that if he could not see Xuanzang, he would follow the example of the kings in history who destroyed the Buddhism, and led his army riding on elephants to smash Nalanda Temple.

Shilabhadra had to let Xuanzang visit King Kuma'ra,

法真谛，使我国家的广大人民受益。现在我此行不虚，很有收获，想回去把这些经书翻译出来，这是对师恩和大家好意最大的报答。"戒贤法师欣喜地说："这也是我所希望你做的。"于是吩咐大家不要再苦留玄奘。

就在这时，鸠摩罗王派来的使者到了，希望戒贤把中国高僧送过去。戒贤担心戒日王要派玄奘去参加辩论会，就回信给鸠摩罗王说："中国僧人决定回国去，来不及到您那儿去了。"鸠摩罗王又派使者来传话说："就算玄奘要回国，先到我那儿一下再走，也没有什么困难，希望这位中国高僧一定光临，不要再拖延了。"戒贤法师拖着不把玄奘送去，鸠摩罗王大怒，又派人送来一封语气极其严厉的信威胁说，如果再不把人送去，他就要效仿历史上那些毁坏佛法的国王，率领骑着大象的军队，把那烂陀寺踏得粉碎。

戒贤只好让玄奘前往鸠摩罗王那里，希望他能够说服鸠摩罗王推行和保护佛教。玄奘跟随使者到了鸠摩罗王那儿，这位国王非常高兴，率领大臣们以尊贵的礼节欢迎他，把他请到宫中，每天以音乐、美食和香花供养他，就这样过了一个来月。玄奘向他描述中国的情形，这位国王悠然神往。在玄奘回国后，唐

hoping Xuanzang could persuade the King to promote and protect Buddhism. Xuanzang followed the messenger to visit the King. The King was very pleased and led his ministers to greet him with distinguished courtesy, and invited him to the palace and treated him with music, feast, and fragrant flowers every day for a month. Xuanzang gave a description of China's situations to the King, fascinating the King leisurely. After Xuanzang returned to his country, the envoys of the Tang Dynasty went to India. King Kuma'ra took the initiative to send people to bring valuables and the map of India to the Tang Dynasty, and requested to get the portrait of Laozi and *Tao Te Ching*.

The year was roughly equivalent to the 14th year (640) of Zhenguan reign of Tang Dynasty (640). King Harshavardhana returned from the battlefield, and was very displeased to hear that Xuanzang was in the palace of the King Kuma'ra, so he sent his envoy to the King Kuma'ra to ask the king to send the Chinese monk back. King Kuma'ra answered, "It is OK if you want to take my head, but the master cannot go back." King Harshavardhana felt it strange how King Kuma'ra could look down upon him in that way, and used such verbal abuse demeaning his identity for a monk. King Harshavardhana sent a messenger to tell King Kuma'ra, "Then please give your head to my messenger and let

《诺距罗尊者图》，相传他原是一名勇猛的战士，后来出家，修成罗汉。
Portrait of Nakula Arhat. It was said he was a brave warrior and became a monk and cultivated himself into Arhat.

朝的使臣出使印度，鸠摩罗王曾主动派人向唐朝献上奇珍异宝和印度地图，并且请求得到老子的画像和《道德经》。

这时候大约相当于唐太宗贞观十四年（640），戒日王打完仗回来，听说玄奘到鸠摩罗王那里去了，很不高兴，就派使者到鸠摩罗王那里，要他赶紧把中国僧人送回来。鸠摩罗王回答说："要我的头可以，但法师不能回去。"戒日王奇怪鸠摩罗王怎么敢这样轻视他，居然为了一个僧人说出这样有失身份的粗话。他又派使者告诉鸠摩罗王说："那就请把你的人头让我的使者带回来吧！"鸠摩罗王知道得罪了戒日王，就下令调集2万象军，乘3万艘船，带上

> ### Laozi and *Tao Te Ching*
>
> Laozi, Li Er, is also known as Lao Dan. Laozi was a respectful title for him. He lived about during the Spring and Autumn Period (770–476 BC). He was a great philosopher and thinker, and the founder of the Taoism in ancient Chinese history. His work *Tao Te Ching*, initially known as Laozi, contains profound and dialectic philosophy. Laozi's philosophy has influenced on China for thousands of years, and also spread to many places outside China. The book has witnessed 1,000-plus foreign versions as the ancient Chinese classics translated with the largest number of languages.

him take it back!" King Kuma'ra knew he had offended King Harshavardhana, so he ordered the mobilization of 20,000 soldiers on elephants to take 30,000 ships along with Xuanzang, and headed for the territory of King Harshavardhana against the Ganges River.

King Kuma'ra took his ministers to meet King Harshavardhana and compromised, so King Harshavardhana turned his rage into gladness. He asked why Xuanzang did not come, and the King Kuma'ra said, "You respect the talents and Buddhism. How can ask the master to meet you?" King Harshavardhana said he would go to visit Xuanzang the next day. After King Kuma'ra returned, he said to Xuanzang he was afraid

老子和《道德经》

老子即李耳,又叫老聃,老子是人们对他的尊称,大约生活于春秋时期(前770—前476)。他是中国古代伟大的哲学家、思想家,道家学派的创始人。他的著作《道德经》起初称为《老子》,含有深邃而富有辩证法的哲学思想。老子的思想影响中国达数千年之久,而且传播到了中国以外的许多地方,其国外版本有1000多种,是被翻译语言最多的中国古代典籍。

玄奘,逆着恒河前往戒日王的领地。

鸠摩罗王带着大臣们去拜见戒日王,向他妥协,戒日王于是转怒为喜。他问玄奘为什么没有跟来,鸠摩罗王说:"大王尊重人才和佛法,怎么能让法师来拜见你呢?"戒日王表示第二天就过去见玄奘。鸠摩罗王回去后,对玄奘说,戒日王恐怕今天晚上就会赶来。半夜时分,戒日王果然来了,河上点起数千支巨大的火炬,他每迈动一步,就有几百面铜鼓同时敲响一下。见面之后,戒日王并没有为难玄奘,礼节很周到,还打听唐王朝的事。这样,戒日王与鸠摩罗王、玄奘之

that King Harshavardhana would come that night. At midnight, King Harshavardhana came indeed, with several thousand huge torches lighting above the river. When he took each step forward, hundreds of drums would sound at the same time. At the meeting, King Harshavardhana did not embarrass Xuanzang. He treated him with very thoughtful etiquettes, and inquired about the Tang Dynasty. In this way, the contradictions between King Harshavardhana and King Kuma'ra & Xuanzang were eliminated.

The next day, King Harshavardhana sent the envoy to take Xuanzang to his palace. He asked for the *Debate on the Evil Opinions*. Upon reading, he showed great appreciation, and said to others monks passing on the Buddhism to him, "I have heard that with sunshine, the faint candlelight like firefly will not be seen; with lightning, the sound like the knocking of the hammer and chisel will not be heard. For the sects and doctrines you are guarding, he refuted, so you can try to save them." As a result, no one dared to challenge. King Harshavardhana's sister was an intelligent woman familiar with Buddhist scriptures, and was a great admirer of Xuanzang's theory. King Harshavardhan said to Xuanzang, although he and the people around him were convinced by his Mahayana theory, Theravada believers in other countries would probably stick to some unknown and ignorant ideas.

间的矛盾就消除了。

第二天，戒日王派使者来将玄奘迎进他的行宫。他索取《破恶见论》阅读，看了之后十分赞赏，对身边其他传授他佛法的僧人说："我听说日光出来，萤火虫一样微弱的烛光就看不到了；天雷轰鸣，像锤子和凿子敲打发出的声音就听不到了。你们所守护的宗派教义，他都驳倒了，你们可试着解救一下。"结果没人敢发表异议。戒日王的妹妹是个聪慧的女人，熟悉佛学经典，她对玄奘的理论也赞赏不已。戒日王对玄奘说，虽然他和他周围的人都信服他的大乘理论，但其他国家信仰小乘的人恐怕还会坚持一些愚昧不明的想法，因此他希望在曲女城举行一次辩论法会，通知五印度的佛教、婆罗门教及其他各种宗教人士，都来听玄奘讲解大乘理论，通过辩论，让其他宗教派别的人不敢再说大乘佛教的坏话。然后，戒日王就这样向各地发布了通知。

这年冬天，玄奘随戒日王回到曲女城。赶来参加大会的有18个国家的国王，3000多名高水平的佛教僧人，2000多名婆罗门教及其他宗教的信徒，那烂陀寺则派出了1000多名僧人参加。加上随从人员、大象和车辆等交

He hoped to hold a debate in the city of Sankasya, and informed Buddhism, Brahmanism, and other religious people in East, South, West, North, and Central India to listen to Mahayana theory to be explained by Xuanzang. The debate enabled people of other religious sects not to dare to speak ill of Mahayana Buddhism. Then, King Harshavardhana issued the notice.

That winter, Xuanzang returned to Sankasya along with King Harshavardhana. The kings of 18 states rushed to participate in the debate, involving more than 3,000 Buddhist monks, more than 2,000 Brahmanism and other religious believers, and more than 100 monks from the Nalanda Temple. Together with the entourage, elephants, carriages, and other transportation, and various articles taken by people, the scene was very spectacular.

On the day when the debate commenced, King Harshavardhana and King Kuma'ra dressed up as Buddhist patron saints, guarding on both sides of a gold statue of Buddha placed on an elephant. Xuanzang and other important figures in the debate rode on the elephant and followed them, followed by other kings, ministers, and eminent monks riding on 300 elephants. Two temporary halls were erected on the debate venue, which could accommodate more than 1,000 people. Those present were King Harshavardhana, Xuanzang et al, and 18 kings, more than 1,000 Buddhist monks, more than

敦煌莫高窟第285窟，菩萨群像绘画
No. 285 Grotto, Dunhuang Mogao Grottos. Painting of Bodhisattva.

通工具、人们携带的各种物品，场面非常壮观。

　　大会开始那天，戒日王和鸠摩罗王扮成佛教守护神的形象，守护在一尊安放在大象身上的金佛像两边。玄奘和其他参加辩论的重要人物坐着大象跟在后

500 Brahmanism and other religious believers, and more than 200 ministers from various states, while other people could only stay outside the gate.

King Harshavardhana asked Xuanzang to sit on the special seat as the primary speaker at the debate to advocate his Mahayana theory and the major contents of *Debate on Evil Opinions*, and ordered a monk from the Nalanda Temple to read the book for everyone present. A book was also hung outside the venue gate. King Harshavardhana announced that if any word in the book did not make sense and could be refuted, Xuanzang would be willing to cut off his head to apologize to everyone. People found that King Harshavardhana intended to support Xuanzang, so from morning to night, no one dared to debate Xuanzang. It was the case the next day and the third day.

On the fifth day, some people of Theravada Buddhism and other religious sects set on a fire secretly wanting to kill Master Xuanzang. Even King Harshavardhana personally participated in the efforts to put out the fire. After the fire was quenched, King Harshavardhana announced that whoever hurt Xuanzang would be beheaded; whoever insulted him would lose his tongue. In this way, evil-minded people did not dare to act rashly. Some 18 days passed, but nobody would dare to challenge. On the last evening, Xuanzang again delivered

面，他们后面是分乘300头大象的其他国王、大臣、高僧。会场搭建了两座临时的大殿，各可以坐1000多人。入场的除了戒日王、玄奘等人外，还有18位国王、1000多位佛教僧人、500多位婆罗门教及其他宗教信徒、200多位各国的大臣，其他人只能在院门外。

敦煌莫高窟第62窟，各国王子听法屏风画
No.62 Grotto, Dunhuang Mogao Grottos. Painting of princess from different countries listening to Buddhist lectures.

a speech, and many people changed their mind to believe in the Mahayana doctrine.

King Harshavardhana ordered to decorate an elephant, and place an umbrella above the elephant, and ask Xuanzang to sit on the elephant accompanied by nobles and ministers to parade in the town, thus declaring his complete victory at the debate. Xuanzang did not want to show off like that, but King Harshavardhana said that it was an old rule and could not be breached. So Xuanzang sat on the elephant to accept congratulations. People burnt incenses and scattered flowers in the streets as lively as festival occasions, and gave a wonderful respectful title to Xuanzang. From then on, Xuanzang's reputation spread around India.

After the debate in the city of Sankasya concluded, Xuanzang bid a farewell to King Harshavardhana and hoped to return to China quickly. But King Harshavardhana asked him to participate in the forthcoming Sixth Unreserved Assembly for Almsgiving. The event, lasting 75 days each time, was held once in every five years, inviting all Indian Buddhist monks, Brahmins and poor people to participate and giving alms of a large number of properties to them. Xuanzang then followed King Harshavardhana to today's Allahabad of Uttar Pradesh in India, and the venue of the assembly was set in an open field between the Ganges River and

戒日王请玄奘作为大会的主讲人坐上特别的座位，宣扬他的大乘理论和《破恶见论》的主要内容，又令一位那烂陀寺的僧人将这部著作读给众人听，另外，会场门外也悬挂了一本。戒日王宣布，如果书里面有一个字写得没有道理，可以被驳倒，玄奘愿意把头砍下来向大家谢罪。人们看出戒日王倾向于玄奘，因此从早到晚，没有一个人敢站出来和玄奘辩论。第二天、第三天也是这样。

到了第五天，有些小乘佛教和其他宗教派别的人暗地里放了一把火，想害死玄奘法师。事起仓促，连戒日王都亲自参加扑火。火被扑灭后，戒日王宣布，若有人伤害玄奘，将被斩首；辱骂他，将被割去舌头，正当的辩论则除外。这一来，有邪恶想法的人也不敢再轻举妄动。18天过去了，始终没有人敢出来挑战。在最后一个晚上，玄奘再次发表演说，许多人纷纷改而信奉大乘教义。

戒日王令人装饰一头大象，在大象身上张起伞盖，请玄奘坐上去，由贵族大臣陪伴，在城里游行，以此宣告他在辩论大会上取得完全的胜利。玄奘不想这样招摇，但戒日王说这是老规矩，不能违背。于

the Jumna River. About half a million people attended the assembly. The assembly was held according to complicated procedures, and finally King Harshavardhana even gave alms of his clothes and accessories, and wore common clothes. Anyway, it was only a symbolic ceremony, and a few days later, other kings would bought back the clothes that King Harshavardhana gave as alms, and gave them to King Harshavardhana.

Xuanzang bid a farewell to King Harshavardhana. King Harshavardhana and King Kuma'ra again and again asked him not to leave. Finally, Xuanzang said to them, "China is very far from here, and Buddhism is introduced relatively late, and it is also incomplete. Therefore, I came to India. Now the people of China are all eager for me to return with Buddhist scriptures. Buddhist scriptures say that those who prevent others from accepting Buddhism will become blind generation by generation. If you force me not to leave, would you not be afraid of eye retribution?" So the two kings did not prevent Xuanzang, and then asked how he would go back. Xuanzang said that he hoped to fulfill his original promise to the King of Gaochang, so he would still return by land in the north. King Harshavardhana et al gave him a large number of properties, but Xuanzang refused, and only accepted a shawl given by King Kum'ra to use as a shelter from the rain on his journey.

是，玄奘就坐上大象，接受人们的祝贺。人们在街上烧香、散花，热闹得像过节一样，并将美好的尊称献给玄奘。从这时候起，玄奘的声誉更是传遍了印度。

曲女城大会结束后，玄奘向戒日王辞行，希望早日回到中国。戒日王请他参加即将举行的第六次无遮大会。这种集会每五年举行一次，每次持续75天，请全印度的佛教僧人、婆罗门和贫困的人参加，将大量财物施舍给他们。玄奘于是跟着戒日王前往钵罗耶迦国（现在印度北方邦的阿拉哈巴德）。无遮大会的会场设在恒河与朱木拿河之间的一大片平整如镜的空地上。参加这次大会的有大约50万人。大会按复杂的程序进行，最后戒日王连身上的衣服、装饰品等都施舍了出去，穿上粗劣的衣服。不过这只是一种象征性的仪式，几天后，其他国王就将戒日王施舍出去的衣物又赎了回来，仍然献给他。

玄奘又向戒日王辞行，戒日王和鸠摩罗王一再挽留他。最后，玄奘向他们说："中国离这里很远，佛法传入比较晚，而且不完备。我就是为这个才来印度的。现在那里的人民都在渴望我带着佛经回去。佛经上说，阻碍别人接受佛法的人会世世代代失明，如果

King Harshavardhana gave Xuanzang an elephant to facilitate transport of Buddhist statues and scriptures. Xuanzang set off along with a king of North India. King Harshavardhana wrote a letter to send several officials to escort Xuanzang and asked them to escort him all the way to the territory of the Tang Dynasty. Although Xuanzang was eager to go back home, he was still reluctant to part from them, bidding an emotional farewell to King Harshavardhana and other officials.

你们强行留下我，难道不怕没有眼睛的报应吗？"两位国王就不好再阻拦玄奘，于是问他怎么回去。玄奘说希望兑现当初对高昌国王的承诺，仍然从北面的陆路回去。戒日王等送给他大量财物，玄奘都不接受，只接受了鸠摩王所送的一条披肩，以备在路上挡雨。

戒日王送给玄奘一头大象，方便装运佛像、经书等。玄奘跟着北印度的一位国王一起上路。戒日王写了亲笔书信，派几位官员护送玄奘，要他们一直送他到唐王朝的领地。玄奘虽然归心似箭，但在分手之际，也有些恋恋不舍，与戒日王等人很动感情地告别。

VII

Eastward Return from a Pilgrimage for Buddhist Scriptures

Probably in the spring of the 17th year (643) of Zhenguan of Emperor Taizong, Xuanzang embarked on his return journey with 657 Buddhist scriptures, many Buddhist statues, and lots of flower and fruit seeds and more. Compared to his pilgrimage to India, his material conditions improved a lot, and he was more experienced and witnessed a smooth journey all the way without particularly dangerous situations.

Some accidents happened on his way. Firstly, he came to North India from Central India, and arrived at the east part and northwest part of today's Pakistan. On that day, he reached Takkasila (now northwest of Rawalpindi in today's Pakistan). He had reached here by crossing the Indus River when he first came to India, now he would cross it. Indus River flow was very rapid with ferocious animals like crocodiles. His companions along with Buddhist scriptures and statues took a boat to cross the river, while Xuanzang rode an elephant to across the river.

7

取经东归

大概在唐太宗贞观十七年（643）春，玄奘携带657部佛经、众多佛教塑像以及许多花果种子等，踏上了返国的旅程。与来时相比，他现在的物质条件改善了很多，经验也更丰富，一路上比较顺利，没有遇到特别危险的情况。

玄奘回国的路上也发生了一些意外。他由中印度先到北印度，来到现在的巴基斯坦东部、西北部地区。这一天，到了呾叉始罗国（现在巴基斯坦的拉瓦尔品第西北），当年他初到印度时就曾渡过印度河来到这里，现在又要渡河过去。印度河水流很急，里面有鳄鱼之类的凶猛动物出没。同伴们与经书、佛像一起坐船，玄奘则骑大象过河，他特意让一个人看护经书和花种子。但是船到河中央时突然起了风浪，船摇晃得快要翻了。守经人不幸落水，虽然众人把他救了上来，但损失了一部分

He specially arranged a person to guard the scriptures and flower seeds. However, they met waves suddenly when the boat was in the middle of the river, and the waves almost capsized the boat. The scripture guardian unfortunately fell into the water. Although he was saved, some scriptures and a lot of flower seeds were lost.

The King of Kapicsa previously came to visit Utakhanda (in the north of today's Attock in Pakistan). At the news that Xuanzang returned, he went to the river to meet Xuanzang. When he learned that Xuanzang had lost some Buddhist scriptures, he told a local legend: whoever takes Indian specialties, famous and valuable flowers and fruits, and sarira to cross the river, his boat will be capsized. He accompanied Xuanzang to the town and stayed at a monastery. At the news, the King of Kasmira also came to visit Xuanzang. The two kings enthusiastically helped Xuanzang. In order to compensate the loss of the scriptures, Xuanzang stayed for some time, and sent for copying Buddhist scriptures collected in Udya'na (now Swat River region of North West Frontier Province in Pakistan).

Xuanzang set off with the King of Kapicsa, and before departure, the King of Kapicsa assigned a minister to lead more than 100 people to escort Xuanzang to a part of the snow-capped mountain in the Hindu Kush Mountain range. After passing the snow-capped mountain, they climbed another high snow mountain with abrupt winds,

鲜花供养的佛像
Buddhist statue, provided with flowers.

经书和很多花种子。

迦毕试的国王此前来到乌铎迦汉荼城（在现在巴基斯坦的阿托克以北）做客，听说玄奘回来了，亲自到河边迎接。他得知玄奘损失了经书，就讲述了当地的一个传说：凡是带着印度的特产、名贵花果及舍利渡河的，就要翻船。他陪着玄奘进城，在一个寺院寄住。迦湿弥罗国的国王闻讯，也赶来看望玄奘。这两位国王都是当年热情帮助过玄奘的人。为了弥补经书的损失，玄奘停留了一段时间，派人去乌仗那国（现

so that even no bird could fly there.

After passing the snow-capped mountains, Xuanzang entered today's Afghanistan. He came to Kondoz again, whose king was still that grandson of Khan of the Turks. He was friendly to Xuanzang, and sent an escort for Xuanzang. Xuanzang was informed that the Kingdom of Gaochang had been eliminated by the Tang Dynasty in the 14th year (640) of Zhenguan period. There was no need for Xuanzang to fulfill his promise to live there for three years, so he had only one idea: return to Chang'an quickly. He adjusted his route, so he did not follow the way he came. He passed through today's Afghanistan's Wakhan Corridor, crossed Congling, and reached Gorbani (now Taxkorgan Tajik Autonomous County of Xinjiang).

On the way to the northeast direction, they met a group of bandits, and as a result, the elephant given to him by King Harshavardhana was chased by bandits and fell into the river and drowned. Xuanzang and his companions walked with difficulty with the Buddhist scriptures, statues and other items, passed through today's Shache, Yecheng, and other places in Xinjiang, and then reached Khotan (now Hotan in Xinjiang). That year was the 18th year (644) of Zhenguan.

Khotan was an independent state at that time, but had a very close relationship with the Tang Dynasty. Buddhism prevailed in Khotan, and at the news that Xuanzang

在巴基斯坦西北边境省的斯瓦特河地区）抄写那里收藏的佛教经书。

玄奘与迦毕试国王结伴而行，分手的时候，迦毕试国王派一个大臣率领100多人，护送玄奘过兴都库什山山脉的一段雪山。过了这道雪山，又登上另一座雪山，山高而风急，连鸟儿在这里都飞不起来。

过了雪山，就进入了现在的阿富汗境内。他又来到活国，这里的国王还是突厥可汗的那个孙子。他对玄奘还比较友好，派人护送玄奘。从他那里，玄奘得知高昌国已于贞观十四年（640）被唐灭亡。玄奘没有必要再去履行在那里住三年的承诺了，他现在只剩下一个想法：赶快回到长安。他调整路线，没有走来时的路，而是途经现在的阿富汗瓦罕走廊，越过葱岭，抵达羯盘陀国（现在新疆的塔什库尔干塔吉克自治县）。

从这里往东北方向的路上，他们遇到了一群强盗，结果戒日王送的那头大象被强盗追赶，掉进水里淹死了。玄奘和同伴很艰难地带着经书、佛像等物品行走，经过现在的新疆莎车、叶城等地，来到了于阗（现在新疆的和田市）。这时是贞观十八年（644）。

would come, the King of Khotan greeted him warmly, and invited him to make a long stay. Xuanzang stayed at Khotan to have a rest. The moment he arrived here, he arranged two things. One was to send for copying scriptures in Kucha and Kashgar (now Kashi in Xinjiang), and the other was to write to the Emperor Taizong of the Tang Dynasty, asking a person of Gaochang to take a message to Chang'an to tell the news of his return. In the letter, he told the Emperor Taizong that he had been to India without approval, gave a brief introduction to his trip, and concluded by saying that the loss of the elephant and the lack of horses and other means of transport caused him to fail to immediately pay a formal visit to the Emperor even though he hoped to see the Emperor immediately. After the messenger left, Xuanzang expounded Buddhist scriptures to Buddhist monks, and the king and general public all loved to listen, attracting more than 1,000 people every day.

Seven or eight months later, he finally saw the envoy sent by Emperor Taizong. The envoy took the Emperor's order to Xuanzang, which wrote, "I am very pleased to know that you went to remote India to seek Buddhism, and now return safe and sound. Please come to see me quickly. You can also take along with you foreign monks who know Sanskrit and Buddhist scripture significance. I have ordered the local governments of Khotan and other

沙漠中的驼队
Camel caravan in desert.

　　于阗这时还是个独立的国家,但与唐王朝的关系非常密切。这里佛教盛行,于阗王听说玄奘到来,热情地迎接他进城,并请他在这里长住。玄奘在于阗停留下来休整。他一到这里,马上安排了两件事,一件是让人到龟兹、疏勒(现在新疆的喀什地区)去抄写经书;另一件就是给唐太宗写了一封信,托一个高昌人带到长安,报告他回来的消息。在这封信里,他向

regions to escort you, and you will not lack of manpower and horses." Xuanzang set off after receiving the order, and the King of Khotan presented him a lot of things and sent him some men to escort him all the way.

Although the environment along the way was similar to that when he originally illegally crossed the border, this time Xuanzang could start his journey openly, and successfully reached Shazhou (now Dunhuang in Gansu province). Emperor Taizong was in Luoyang at that time, asking the minister Fang Xuanling in Chang'an to be responsible for receiving Xuanzang. Xuanzang heard that Emperor Taizong could soon lead his troops for expedition, so he hurried on his way day and night. When he rushed to the Caohe River in the west of Chang'an, the officials did not know and no one showed up to greet him. But many local people knew that he came back, they all hurried to see him. With so many people, the road was blocked so that Xuanzang had no way to move forward, and he had to stay by the Caohe River. It was already the first lunar month of the 19th year (645) of Zhenguan, when Xuanzang was 44 years old.

Fang Xuanling arranged a grand welcome ceremony to greet Xuanzang along with the Buddhist scriptures and statues to Chang'an. All of these things brought back by Xuanzang were on the backs of 20 horses. The government ordered to deliver these things to various

唐太宗说明自己当年是未经许可偷跑到印度的，又简单介绍了他的行程，最后表示，因为失去了大象、缺少马匹等交通工具，虽然他很想马上拜见皇帝，但无法很快赶到。送信的人走后，玄奘就在于阗给佛教僧人们讲解佛经，国王和一般民众也都很爱听，每天都有上千人来听讲。

过了七八个月，他终于等来了唐太宗派出的使者。使者带着皇帝给玄奘的命令，里面说："听说你到遥远的印度访求佛法，现在平安归来，我特别高兴，请你赶快来跟我相见。外国僧人们懂得梵文和佛经意义的，你都可以随便带来。我已命令于阗等地的官府护送你，人手和马匹等都不会缺少。"玄奘接到这道命令后马上动身，于阗王送了他很多东西，并派人一路护送。

虽然一路上的环境跟当初偷越国境时差不多，但这次玄奘可以光明正大地赶路，很顺利地到达了沙州（现在甘肃省的敦煌）。唐太宗当时在洛阳，让留守长安的大臣房玄龄负责接待玄奘。玄奘听说唐太宗可能很快要带兵出征，就日夜兼程地赶路。当他赶到长安城西边的漕河边上时，政府的人还不知道，没有人来迎接。但许多当地人知道他回来了，都赶来观看。

Chinese lunar calendar

Lunar calendar has long been used in China, and is still in use along with solar calendar. Also known as the Chinese calendar and traditional Chinese calendar, it is actually a kind of lunisolar calendar. Generally a year is divided into 12 months with a month of 30 or 29 days. The annual number of days is 11 days less than that of a solar year, so seven leap months are established in 19 years, so that the year with a leap month has 13 months in total. Also according to the location of the sun, a solar year is divided into 24 solar terms so as to guide agricultural planting and other activities.

temples for display, and then brought to Hongfu Temple the next day. The monks of various temples were all happy and dressed themselves neatly, and took out the most beautiful ornaments and utensils. The streets in the city and the long road to the Hongfu Temple were jammed with people, eager to see Xuanzang back from his pilgrimage to India to seek Buddhist scriptures and the Buddhist scriptures and statues he brought back. The government was afraid of a stampede, so it ordered people not to move, and they could stand still to watch and celebrate. As a result, in and outside of the city were the incense smoke and voice of scripture recitation.

A few days later, Xuanzang went to Luoyang to pay a

中国农历

中国长期使用的传统历法，目前仍与公历并行使用，也称为阴历、夏历，其实是阴阳历的一种。一般每年分为12个月，大月30天，小月29天。由于每年的天数比太阳年约差11天，所以在19年里设置7个闰月，有闰月的年份全年13个月。又根据太阳的位置，把一个太阳年分成二十四个节气，以指导农业种植等活动。

因为观看的人太多，堵塞了道路，玄奘无法前进，晚上只好住在漕河边上。这时已经是贞观十九年（645）中国农历的一月，玄奘这一年44岁。

房玄龄安排了盛大的迎接仪式，将玄奘和他带回的佛经、佛像等迎进长安城。玄奘带回的这些东西，用20匹马驮着。官府下令，先将这些东西分送到各个寺院去展览，然后第二天再集中送到弘福寺。各个寺的僧侣们都很欢喜，穿得整整齐齐，将最华丽的装饰品和用具都拿了出来。从城里的大街到弘福寺的几十里路上，街两边都站满了人，争着观看西天归来的玄奘和他取回来的经书、佛像。官府怕发生踩踏事故，

玄奘取经归来，僧侣与信徒们在长安的寺院前迎接他。
When Xuanzang returned with Buddhist scriptures, monks and disciples are greeting him in front of the temple of Chang'an.

formal visit to the Emperor Taizong. He was asked about the places he had traversed, which had not been recorded by anyone before Xuanzang. He could answer the emporer's questions freely as he had been very attentive wherever he traveled. Emperor Taizong was very satisfied, and suggested that he write a book dedicated what he had seen and heard on his journey. Emperor Taizong felt that Xuanzang was very talented, so he advised Xuanzang not to be a monk any longer, and asked him to help govern the country, but Xuanzang declined. Emperor Taizong invited Xuanzang to join him to take his troops on an expedition, but Xuanzang also gently refused. In accordance with the provisions of Buddhism, monks should refrain from such things as wars.

The translation of the Buddhist scriptures was a matter

命令民众不许移动,只能就地观看和庆祝。于是,城里城外到处都是烧香形成的烟云和念诵佛经的声音。

过了几天,玄奘到洛阳去拜见唐太宗。唐太宗问起他路上所走过的地方,这些都是前人没有记载过的,而玄奘因为亲自游历过,每到一处又非常留意,所以应答如流。唐太宗非常满意,建议他专门写一本书来记录这些沿途的见闻。唐太宗觉得玄奘很有才干,就劝他不要再做僧人,来帮助自己治理国家,玄奘委婉地推辞了。唐太宗邀请他跟自己一起带着军队出征,玄奘也委婉地拒绝了。按佛教的规定,僧人应该回避战争这样的场面。

翻译佛经是玄奘特别关心的事情,他请求到河南嵩山的少林寺翻译佛经,因为那里很安静。唐太宗让他住在长安城的弘福寺,说那儿也很安静。玄奘担心会有很多看热闹的人,就请唐太宗派人看守寺院的门。唐太宗很愉快地答应了,并指示政府有关部门协助玄奘完成翻译佛经的工作。

玄奘从洛阳回到长安,住进弘福寺,向政府要求配备各方面的翻译助手。过了几个月,数十名从全国各个寺院选拔出来的优秀人才集中到了弘福寺。玄奘

of particular concern to Xuanzang, who requested that he do his translation work of the Buddhist scriptures in Songshan Shaolin Temple in Henan, for it was a very quiet place. Emperor Taizong let him stay at the Hongfu Temple in Chang'an, saying it was also very quiet. Xuanzang was worried that a lot of curious people would come by, so he asked Emperor Taizong to assign guards to keep watch over the gate of the temple. Emperor Taizong agreed quite happily, and instructed relevant government departments to assist Xuanzang with the translation.

Xuanzang returned to Chang'an from Luoyang, and stayed at Hongfu Temple. He asked the government to give him translation assistants in various aspects. A few months later, dozens of outstanding talented monks selected from monasteries across the country came to Hongfu Temple. Xuanzang served as a translator of the major works, and his assistants would be responsible for either negotiating with him on the translation contents, connecting translations into fluent articles, recording translations, copying, checking the accuracy of the Sanskrit, and so on. Xuanzang immediately got down to work with these assistants. The translation of some short scriptures was finished in a day, while it took a few days for some, and even until the end of the year. Xuanzang gave the translated scriptures to Emperor Taizong.

Of course, he did not forget the book that Emperor

考虑得很周密，他担任主要翻译工作，助手们有的负责与他商定译文的内容，有的负责将译文连接成通顺的文句，有的负责记录译文，有的负责抄写，还有人负责核对所读的梵文是不是准确，等等。玄奘与这些助手马上开始进行翻译工作，有些短的经文当天就译完了，有的过了几天才译完，有的直到年底才译完。玄奘把这些译好的经文陆续献给唐太宗。

当然，他没有忘记唐太宗建议他写的那本书，那也是这位雄才大略的皇帝迫切想看到的书。几乎与翻译佛经同时，他开始撰写记录沿途见闻的《大唐西域记》。这本书由他口述，他的学生辩机笔录，花了一年多的时间，到贞观二十年（646）的秋天，他完成了这部十多万字的著作。中国古代文言以简洁著称，十多万字是一个很惊人的篇幅。

这本书详细记载了他离开高昌以后的行踪，把他亲自到过的110个和听别人谈到的28个国家、城邦、地区各方面的情况都作了介绍。书中涉及的地域几乎包括现在所说的中亚和南亚地区。这些地区7世纪前的的历史和地理资料流传极少，尤其是古代印度的历史，几乎是一片空白。要想了解7世纪前的印度，《大唐西

Taizong suggested he write, and that was also the book the ingenious emperor was eager to see. Nearly simultaneously with the translation of Buddhist scriptures, he began to write *On Yuan Chwang's Travels in India*, a book to record what he had seen and heard during his journey. He narrated and his student Bianji took the stories down in writing. For more than a year until the autumn of the 20th year (646) of Zhenguan period, he completed the book with more than 100,000 Chinese characters. Ancient classical Chinese language was well-known for its conciseness, so a book with more than 100,000 classical Chinese characters is really amazing.

This book has detailed records of his whereabouts after leaving Gaochang, covering the introduction to the 110 states he personally visited and another 28 states and regions he heard about from others. The places in the book include nearly all of today's Central Asia and South Asia regions. There is only a small amount of historical and geographical information before the 7th century, especially the history of ancient India, which is almost nonexistent. The book is nearly the only reliable documentation to understand India in the 7th century. Scholars researching modern history, philosophy history, literature history, and history of political thoughts of Central Asia and South Asia cannot do without the book. In fact, this is the work of Xuanzang most well-known to people.

域记》几乎就是唯一可靠的文献资料。近现代从事中亚和南亚历史、哲学史、文学史、政治思想史等方面研究的学者，都离不开这本书。事实上，这也是玄奘最为人熟知的作品。

近现代的考古学家依据这本书的记载，成功地发掘了许多古老文化的遗址：呾叉始罗的废墟、王舍城的旧址、鹿野苑的古寺、那烂陀寺的遗迹，等等。印度著名历史学家马宗达在他的著作《古代印度》中赞美说："我们记述的有关戒日王的绝大部分事实都来自一个（中国）游方僧的惊人的记载，此外，这些记载还给我们描绘了一幅印度当时情况的图画，这种图画

大雁塔远景
Distant view of Dayan Pagoda.

Contemporary and modern archaeologists have succeeded in the excavation of many ancient cultural relics according to the records in the book, for example, ruins of Taxila, site of Rajagrha, ancient temple of Sarnath, and ruins of Nalanda Temple. Majumdar, a famous Indian historian, praised in his book *Ancient India*, "The overwhelming majority of facts about the King Harshavardhana we documented derive from the amazing records of a (Chinese) monk. Besides, these records also give us a description of the picture of India at that time, and it cannot be found in any other place."

Xuanzang himself was most concerned about the translation of Buddhist scriptures. For the about two decades, from his return to China to his death, he led his students to engage in the translations. He had plans for translating those Buddhist scriptures he brought back, which not only enriched the treasure house of the Chinese culture, but also preserved precious historical materials for India. He was very strict in the translation, and drafted up to 10 procedures for the translation division, which were to guarantee a high-quality translation. He spent more than two years translating *Yogacara-bhumi-sastra*, and presented it to Emperor Taizong. After winning the praise of Emperor Taizong, he took the opportunity to request the Emperor to write a preface to his translation. Emperor Taizong agreed, and wrote a preface with 781 Chinese

是任何地方都找不到的。"

玄奘本人最关注的还是翻译佛经的事业。他回到中国之后，直到去世为止的约20年时间，几乎都在带领学生们从事翻译工作。他有计划地翻译带回的佛经，不仅丰富了中国的文化宝库，也为印度保存了珍贵史料。他译经的态度非常严谨，由他拟定的分工合作的翻译程序多达十道，保证了译文的高水准。他花了两年多时间译出篇幅很大的《瑜伽师地论》，将它献给唐太宗。在得到唐太宗的夸赞后，他趁机请求皇帝为他翻译的经书写一篇序文。唐太宗答应了，亲自动手写了一篇781个字的序文，作为所有经书的总序。唐太宗等皇帝的支持，保证了玄奘的翻译工作受到最大保护。

贞观二十二年（648）冬天，在皇太子、后来的唐高宗李治（628—683）的主持下，一座新的宏大寺院慈恩寺建成了。玄奘奉命搬进这里，继续他的翻译事业。当时唐太宗已到晚年，健康状况不佳，开始信奉佛教，经常要求玄奘陪伴他，听他讲解佛法和取经路上的见闻，并叹息说："我遇到法师的时候太晚了，来不及使佛教更加兴盛。"玄奘白天陪皇帝谈话，晚上回到寺院

characters as the general foreword to all the scriptures. The support offered by Emperor Tang Taizong and other emperors ensured the greatest protection of the translation of Xuanzang.

Presided over by Li Zhi, Crown Prince and later Emperor Gaozong (628–683), a new grand temple, Cien Temple was completed in the winter of the 22nd year (648) of Zhenguan period. Xuanzang was ordered to move there, and continue his translation career. In the late years, Emperor Taizong was in poor health, and began to believe in Buddhism, often requiring Xuanzang to accompany him, and listening to his expounding over Buddhism and his stories on his journey. The emporer said with a sigh, "Master, I met you too late to make Buddhism more predominant." Xuanzang talked with the emperor during the daytime, and returned at night to continue his translation of Buddhist scriptures.

Before long, Emperor Taizong passed away. Xuanzang felt the relentlessness of the times. In order to do more translation, he set himself to the task every day. In case his translation was delayed at daytime, he would certainly work overtime to make up for the lost time. He strictly observed the various precepts of Buddhism, and meanwhile, he was also responsible for giving lectures to monks who sought learning, and managing all kinds of affairs of the temple.

里继续翻译佛经。

不久，唐太宗就去世了。玄奘感到岁月的无情，为了完成更多的翻译工作，他给自己规定了每天的任务，如果白天有事情耽误了翻译，晚上一定加班弥补完成。他严格遵守佛教的各种戒律，同时还要负责给求学的僧人们讲课，并管理寺院里的种种事务。

唐高宗永徽三年（652），玄奘已经超过50岁了。他担心从印度带回来的佛经遭遇散失、火灾等灾难，就请皇帝批准他在慈恩寺的西院造一座塔来存放这些经书。玄奘亲自带着工具搬运土石，带领众人很快修成了这座塔。这座塔的外形与中国传统的塔不太一样，有人认为，它很可能模仿了印度那烂陀寺附近山上的那座大雁塔。可惜的是，这座塔质量不太好，30年后就塌了。女皇帝武则天（624—705）重修了这座塔，正式命名它为大雁塔。这座塔后来又经过多次重新修建，现在仍立在西安市的慈恩寺里。

玄奘回到中国后，印度的朋友们并没有忘记他。就在他修造大雁塔之后不久，一位印度僧人法长来到长安。玄奘在印度时有两位经常一起讨论佛学问题的友人智光、慧天，法长与他们是一个寺院的，他带来

In the 3rd year (652) of Emperor Gaozong of Tang Dynasty, Xuanzang was more than 50 years old. He was concerned that the Buddhist scriptures brought back from India might suffer from loss, fire, and other disasters, so he asked the emperor to approve the building of a pagoda in the west courtyard of the Cien Temple to preserve these scriptures. Xuanzang himself took tools to move earth and rocks, and led other people to complete the pagoda quickly. The outline of the pagoda is different from that of traditional Chinese pagodas, and some thought it was likely a mimic of that pagoda on the mountain nearby Indian Nalanda Temple. Unfortunately, the pagoda was not of very good quality, and collapsed three decades later. Empress Wu (624–705) rebuilt it, and officially named it the Giant Wild Goose Pagoda. Rebuilt many times later, the pagoda still stands at the Cien Temple in Xi'an.

After Xuanzang returned to China, his friends in India did not forget him. Shortly after he built the Giant Wild Goose Pagoda, an Indian monk, who was at the same temple in India with two friends of Xuanzang, Jnanaprabha and Prajnadeva, with whom Xuanzang often talked about Buddhism issues, reached Chang'an with letters and a gift from them. The gift was only two rolls of white cotton cloth, but as a Chinese saying put it, "The gift sent from afar, as light as a goose feather, conveys deep affections." His friends missing him still moved Xuanzang

大雁塔近景
Near view of Dayan Pagoda.

Cien Temple and Giant Wild Goose Pagoda

Cien Temple is a famous Chinese Buddhist temple located in Xi'an, Shaanxi province. In the 20th year of Zhenguan period of the Tang Dynasty, the Crown Prince Li Zhi expanded an old temple into Cien Temple to commemorate his mother. Xuanzang was ordered to preside over the translation of Buddhist scriptures at the temple. In the 3rd year of the Yonghui period, Xuanzang built the Giant Wild Goose Pagoda in the temple with Tang Emperor's approval, and used the pagoda to preserve Buddhist scriptures, statues, and sariras. The pagoda was rebuilt several times, and the existing seven-story pagoda is 64.5 meters high. The Giant Wild Goose Pagoda is a famous Chinese ancient architecture, and now regarded as a symbol of the ancient capital Xi'an.)

greatly. Two years later, when the monk intended to return to India, Xuanzang wrote a note to his friends, and sent that, along with gifts, back to his two friends.

Xuanzang spend his last four years of life translating long *Mahaprajnaparamita-sutra*. The Sanskrit edition covers 200,000 verses, making all his students afraid of the incredible length, and they hoped to translate only the abridged edition. But Xuanzang decided to translate the whole text. He translated it into up to 600 volumes in Chinese with amazing perseverance. He was very worried

慈恩寺与大雁塔

慈恩寺是著名中国佛教寺院，位于现在陕西省西安市。唐贞观二十二年，皇太子李治为纪念他的母亲，将一座旧寺院扩建成为慈恩寺。后来玄奘奉命在这里主持翻译佛经。永徽三年，经唐高宗批准，玄奘在寺内里修建了大雁塔，用来保存佛经、佛像、舍利等。这座塔后来经过多次改建，现存塔共有7层，高64.5米。大雁塔是中国著名的古代建筑，现在被视为古都西安的象征。

了那两位友人的信件和礼物。虽然礼物只是两匹白棉布，但正如中国人所说，"千里送鹅毛，礼轻情义重"，朋友的惦念还是很让玄奘感动。两年后法长要回印度，玄奘写了回信并附上礼物，请法长带给两位朋友。

玄奘生命的最后四年，全部用来翻译篇幅极大的《大般若经》。这部经书梵文本有20万颂，学生们都很畏惧，希望删节之后再译。玄奘考虑再三，还是决定全文翻译。他以惊人的毅力将这部著作翻译成多达600卷的中文。他非常担心这部经书还没有译完，自

that he would die before the completion of the translation. When all the translation work was completed, he felt very pleased. A few months later, in the spring of the first year (664) of Linde of Emperor Gaozong, the eminent monk died at the age of 63.

Perseverant in his beliefs and diligent with noble personality, the Chinese monk went on a long pilgrimage to India for Buddhist scriptures, leaving rich thoughts and cultural heritage for later generations. These words come from *India and China* written by an Idian historian: "Among many Chinese people who visited India, Xuanzang is undoubtedly the greatest. He is a symbol of Sino-Indian cultural cooperation."

己就已去世。当全部翻译工作完成之时,他感到很欣慰。几个月后,即唐高宗麟德元年(664)的二月间,这位高僧走完了他的人生,享年63岁。

这位西天取经的中国僧人坚持信仰、高尚勤奋,为了理想而远赴印度取经,为后人留下了丰富的思想和文化遗产。正如拉德利西南著《印度与中国》所说:"在到过印度的许多中国人之中,玄奘无疑是最伟大的一个。他是中印文化合作的象征。"